A
NEW DAY
IN THE
CITY

DONNA CLAYCOMB SOKOL & L. ROGER OWENS
WITH FOREWORD BY JAMES A. HARNISH

A NEW DAY IN THE CITY

URBAN CHURCH REVIVAL

Abingdon Press
Nashville

A NEW DAY IN THE CITY:
URBAN CHURCH REVIVAL

Library of Congress Cataloging-in-Publication Data has been requested.

ISBN: 978-1-5018-1888-2

A number of the stories in this book began as short articles first published in *Faith & Leadership*. www.faithandleadership.com.

Scripture quotations unless noted otherwise noted are from the Common English Bible. Copyright © 2011 by the Common English Bible. All rights reserved. Used by permission. www.CommonEnglishBible.com.

17 18 19 20 21 22 23 24 25 26—10 9 8 7 6 5 4 3 2 1
MANUFACTURED IN THE UNITED STATES OF AMERICA

For the people, past and present, of
Mount Vernon Place United Methodist Church
and
Duke Memorial United Methodist Church

CONTENTS

CONTENTS

FOREWORD

By James A. Harnish

T his book is a story of hope for mainline, long-established, urban churches: not the mythical hope of returning to glory days in the past, but realistic hope for a new and different future. At the same time, it offers a witness of hope and a pattern for renewal that is applicable to any congregation in any community that wants to take seriously the changing realities of the culture in which we live.

Mount Vernon Place United Methodist and Duke Memorial United Methodist were like hundreds of mainline congregations in cities across our nation. They had grand histories and equally grand, old buildings that were seriously showing their age. Aging members in both congregations remembered the "glory days" when their pews were filled, their choirs were glorious, their children's programs were bursting at the seams, and they were held in high regard by the city around them. But by the time Donna and Roger arrived on the scene, those memories were gathering dust like the faded pictures, neglected choir robes, discarded membership rolls, and unused silver tea service in their closets.

Realizing that the glory days weren't coming back, the aging members at Mount Vernon Place had decided to use up their endowment fund, lock the doors, and turn the keys over to the annual conference. Some people told Roger and Donna to see what they could do, but not many people held out much hope for the future. However, there were faithful people in both congregations who had not given up on the future of their church.

Donna and Roger had read the books on congregational transformation and had attended leadership conferences that emphasized the importance of "visionary leaders" who capture God's vision for the future and relentlessly lead their congregation in its direction. But they soon discovered that much of what they learned simply wouldn't work in their settings, and some of it was more clearly rooted in the Harvard Business School than in the gospel. They also realized that strategic planning tends to assume stability that no longer exists in the constantly changing realities of the world around us.

As one who has tried (sometimes succeeding and sometimes failing) to give that kind of leadership to the congregations I've served, I found their description of "living as explorers on the landscape of God's kingdom, letting that landscape shape our life together and our witness in the world" to be a refreshing, liberating, and hope-filled word for both clergy and lay leadership in any local church.

The process of transformation they offer in this book is grounded in Jesus's vision of the kingdom of God. It led them (and can lead others) in a distinctively God-centered way of being the Body of Christ that is open to adaptation and change.

John Bunyan said, "Hope has a thick skin and will endure many a blow...for the joy that is set before it." This is a story of hope with a thick skin. Transformation is not for the faint of heart. There are no shortcuts, no quick fixes, no simple solutions.

The seven critical conversations Donna and Roger recommend demand an often painful, ruthlessly honest, and boldly faithful commitment that is nothing short of Jesus's warning that unless a grain of wheat go in the ground and die, it will abide alone. But if it dies, it will bring forth new fruit. Consistent with Jesus's parable of the vine, pruning is always painful, but it is the only way for new life to grow.

Donna and Roger know better than to offer easy solutions, but they do provide practical guidance for church leaders who join them in searching for the fulfillment of God's promise of a future with hope for their congregations. They model the importance of asking the right questions that open the way for the Spirit to lead us to fresh answers. Congregational leaders who follow their guidance will make fresh discoveries that will lead them to a new future.

Having served churches in both the exploding suburbs of Orlando and the urban core of Tampa, I agree with their conviction that "no churches are better positioned to rediscover the one focus of God's mission—thus re-uniting mission and evangelism in a single kingdom vision—than urban churches with their opportunity to creatively address so many human needs, including the need for faith in Christ." God still calls us to "seek the welfare of the city...for in its welfare you will find your welfare" (Jer 29:7). God hasn't given up on the city, and neither can we!

The hope in this story is best captured when they say, "We are on an adventure; the destination is unknown, but the joy and the power and the fruit will come with how we live along the way."

I'm grateful that they have invited all of us to join them in this adventure! The challenge is not just to read about their adventure, but to join them on it!

PREFACE

Moving to a new but familiar city on my thirty-third birthday was never part of my plan. There were other places I (Donna) would have rather been on my birthday, with the arms of my boyfriend coming to mind first. And yet, there was a sense that moving back to Washington, DC, was all part of a design put in place decades ago.

I was excited at last to arrive in the place that triggered a two-page vision I tucked away in my purse. I had not been able to stop dreaming about ministry in downtown DC since the district superintendent had shared with me, over three baskets of chips with salsa and salad on the side, a few details about the congregation.

"It's an elderly congregation that has dwindled down to about fifty active members," he said. "Those still there are very committed." He continued,

> Your core group of leaders are all in their nineties. The chair of the personnel committee is ninety-seven, the lay leader is ninety years old, and the feisty chair of finance is ninety-two. The staff is rather large, anchored by a full-time minister of music who has been at the church for more than thirty years.
>
> The building is in total disrepair. Part of it is filled with a consuming stench as water has seeped in over the years. About one-quarter of the facility is unusable.
>
> There is currently a relationship with the Chinese Community Church. Your 11:00 a.m. worship hour is shared with this other

congregation, so you only get to preach every other week as the Chinese pastor preaches the other weeks. Neither congregation is growing. Both have declined since coming together.

Things are not good, Donna. If you are appointed to this church, it will be the hardest thing you have ever done and possibly the hardest thing you will ever do.

But…

My introduction to Mount Vernon Place United Methodist Church started with these words. I had lived in Washington for four years in the 1990s when I served as a White House intern before working on Capitol Hill for both a member of Congress and a United States Senator. I knew the city, and my best friends were still working in the city. But I never dreamed of returning to Washington—especially as a pastor.

Still, I felt a remarkable pull to this place. I knew beyond a shadow of a doubt that God was calling me to guide a process of transformation that would allow a declining church to grow again.

But where would we begin?

I began by signing up for a congregational development event where the workshop offerings made it feel like if I selected the appropriate choices, then I could return home with the exact wisdom I needed to turn the church around, as if ordering three courses from a menu would add up to a memorable meal. But I quickly realized that what worked in other places didn't work as well in downtown Washington, DC. I also learned that there was no one-size-fits-all approach to leading a congregation through renewal.

It's tempting to believe someone has the answers we need. A recently admitted seminary student once called the office to ask, "When we were at your church a couple of weeks ago, I heard the story of how you've been able to really grow a church, stopping decades of decline. Can you tell me how?" If only the answer to the question was as simple as a recipe for chocolate chip cookies. It's not.

When Roger called me a couple of years ago to suggest we write a book together, I was eager to tell the story of transformation I had seen after ten years at Mount Vernon Place. Roger and his wife led similar transformation at Duke Memorial United Methodist Church, an urban church in Durham, North Carolina. Now Roger studies and teaches congregation leadership at Pittsburgh Theological Seminary. Together it seemed we might be able to offer urban congregations a way forward in a climate where transformation-by-recipe doesn't work. We don't have all the answers—no one does—but we have learned a few things along the way and pray this book will be a useful guide and a catalyst for those seeking renewal in their congregations.

INTRODUCTION

F rederick Buechner wrote, "Dreams of fame and fortune die hard, if they ever die at all."[1] Many urban congregations remember the days of fame and fortune, days when their prominent downtown mattered. Population shifts, the decline of congregations, and demographic changes have robbed many downtown churches of these dreams—but not all churches. Some congregations struggle to survive while others are positioned to thrive. Some church buildings have been turned into art museums and coffee shops, and sometimes the barista creating a cappuccino is an employee of a church that has imagined itself in new ways.

We pastored urban congregations that managed to grow again, reversing decades of decline. For the past eleven years, Donna has been the pastor of Mount Vernon Place United Methodist Church in Washington, DC. Roger, with his wife Ginger Thomas, were the copastors of Duke Memorial United Methodist Church in Durham, North Carolina, for five years. Over these periods of time, each of these congregations learned to let go of their nostalgic dreams and tired habits and walk with God into a new day of vibrancy, mission, and ministry.

In *A New Day in the City*, we share the stories of these two churches and many more, and the lessons we ourselves have learned from experience and from studying the leadership of others, in order to help fellow pastors and congregations escape the whirlpool of decline and join God in the deep and wide mission of embodying the kingdom. Along the way, we challenge some of the typical clichés about church leadership, offering a fresh perspective on what congregational renewal can look like and how it can become a reality.

This book doesn't offer easy answers, because churches that need to adapt and change to thrive can't simply replicate what someone else has done or is doing. Rather, we offer the framework for seven crucial conversations urban churches need to have to find their own way to renewal:

1. The process of pruning or letting go

2. An invitation to rethink vision

3. Ways to rethink strategy

4. How to overcome the divide that's created between mission and evangelism

5. How excellence can and should be embodied in a few key ways

6. Thoughts on worship

7. How the pastor, staff, and laity can more effectively work together

Pastors and laity must wrestle and pray about these seven topics—critical issues for urban congregations that want to thrive. Each chapter explores why that issue is crucial and how we need to think differently about it, especially given the realities of urban congregations.

Since we hope you will be reading this book with others—groups of pastors, church staff, or pastors, staff, and lay leaders together—we've included suggestions for conversation called "Discuss This" and suggestions for experimentation called "Try This" in each chapter.

This book is meant to inspire you to take next steps, to widen the conversation, to bring as many people as possible into dreaming about, praying for, and living into renewal in your congregation. An appendix, Hosting Renewal Conversations, is a short guide to how you can use this book to foster renewal where it matters most—right where you are, in the congregation you love. We also pray denominational leaders who are tempted to offer a quick fix can find inspiration in how best to lead and guide congregations. In fact, our prayer throughout our writing is that we could offer pastors, congregations, and denominational leaders helpful thoughts, stories, and ideas about how to bring about new life within existing congregations, particularly in urban settings that are experiencing great change today.

William Sloane Coffin once wrote, "Most church boats don't like to be rocked; they prefer to lie at anchor rather than go places in stormy seas. But that's because we Christians view the Church as the object of our love instead of the subject and instrument of God's. Faith cannot be passive; it has to go forth—to assault the conscience, excite the imagination. Faith fans the flames of creativity altogether as much as it banks the fires of sin."[2]

Some will resist your invitations. Several people may become uncomfortable or even defensive when asked to respond to the questions we encourage you to consider. But we beg you to stop believing that a church that is declining in calm waters is more faithful than a church willing to risk much—or risk it all—by venturing out into a sea of uncertainty. We have witnessed the incredible gifts that come with risk-taking, letting go, trying something new, and seeing things in a different light. We would not trade the journey or where our congregations are now for anything.

BEFORE THE GROWTH, THE PRUNING SHEARS

DAY ONE

The church secretary insisted that I (Donna) take a tour of the church's property on my first day as the new pastor. The tour started on the second floor of the 1958 educational wing that was constructed when the congregation was one of the largest in the nation's capital with a membership roster of more than 4,500 people. Designed to house the educational needs of hundreds of adults and children who journeyed downtown each week, a designated Sunday school class remained for the few dozen individuals who continued to participate. Antique wooden placards hung on most of the doors, even though the secretary explained that only two classes remained while the other classrooms sat empty, collecting clutter.

We peeked inside the rooms and kept walking until we reached an office labeled "Membership" where a two-foot tall vintage Rolodex sat as the centerpiece of a large desk. "Every church member has a card," the secretary shared. "Mary comes in once a week to update the records." I listened to the words while wondering how a church that had not received a new member in the last two years could need someone to update its records weekly. I knew the average age of the fifty or so remaining active members of the congregation was eighty-two, but were that many members dying each week?

We next visited the offices of the Chinese Community Church, a church that started in our historic building in 1935 before purchasing a nearby townhouse for their afternoon worship in 1939. With Chinatown's development a few blocks away, the congregation of the Chinese Community Church continued to grow until it maximized its space, while our congregation declined, leaving plenty of empty space. It seemed like a match made in heaven for the two congregations to come together. A partnership was formed in 1994, and the two congregations shared the building and Sunday morning worship until 2006. The relationship with the Chinese Community Church kept the doors of our church open as the burden associated with operating a large property was evenly divided. Their presence also enabled our congregation to ignore and sometimes deny our dwindling membership and ministry.

The next stop was the music suite where there were piles of sheet music printed on paper that had turned yellow, in addition to boxes of records the choir had produced in the 1950s and 1960s. The music ministry had changed throughout the years, but it was still being anchored by six professional singers who were paid to sing every Sunday.

The property tour ended with a stop at the Undercroft Auditorium where audiences were still gathering for performances throughout the year. When the theatre was first used for plays and musicals, every performer was a church member or active participant. It was a ministry that effectively reached new people. While the current paid director was a member of the church, the actors were only inside the church building for rehearsal or a performance. Drama was a "ministry" the church was proud of and sustained by investing significant financial resources, but one that was not bringing new people into the church or guiding people into a deeper walk of discipleship.

The tour that I allocated fifteen minutes had consumed the entire morning, along with a healthy measure of my self-esteem and optimism. The challenge of reversing decades of decline was larger than I could have ever imagined. The congregation would need to let go of nearly everything it had—stuff crammed in closets and rooms, activities labeled as "ministry" on the back of a bulletin, and several paid staff members. But no one could see the necessary changes yet but me.

It was not only the presence of another congregation that prevented our congregation from facing our current reality, but a million-dollar endowment also enabled the congregation to feel as though we could do whatever we wanted to do since we could afford it. I was told often, "Pastor, it's our money. We voted to spend it. When the money is gone, we are going to close the doors and walk away." The congregation of fifty active members was giving $120,000 a year in tithes and offerings and taking an additional $250,000 from the principal of the endowment that year to meet the financial commitments and ministry priorities, a rate of spending that would leave the congregation bankrupt in four years. Ushering in a different budget became a top priority, and I soon found myself in conflict with the ninety-two-year-old chairperson of the finance committee. We had to let go.

LET IT GO

In their book *The Practice of Adaptive Leadership*, Ronald Heifetz, Alexander Grashow, and Marty Linsky write, "Unlike known or routine problem solving for which past ways of thinking, relating, and operating are sufficient for achieving good outcomes, adaptive work demands three very tough, human tasks: figuring out what to conserve from past practices, figuring out what to discard from past practices, and inventing new ways that build from the best of the past."[1]

Perhaps no greater challenge is posed to congregations today than discerning what to conserve and what to discard as we seek to build upon the best of the past and move into God's intended future. While we may know what needs to be discarded, efforts at letting go often prove futile—if they're even attempted in the first place. Like a young child who wants to take several books and toys on a trip, leaving no room in his suitcase for the clothing he actually needs, congregations have an uncanny ability of seeking to move forward while lugging everything with them whether it's the stuff that fills once-used Sunday school classrooms, the list of activities printed in the calendar on the back of a bulletin, or the paid staff that were needed when a congregation was four times its current size. Given our track record of struggling to let go, it is no wonder Jesus sought to teach people how to grow living things, offering a lesson in pruning when he was first forming groups of disciples.

> I am the true vine, and my Father is the vineyard keeper. He removes any of my branches that don't produce fruit, and he trims any branch that produces fruit so that it will produce even more fruit. (John 15:1-2)

If you want a quick and effective lesson in pruning, purchase a petunia plant for your porch. The plant will be in full bloom when you first bring it home from the nursery, with no signs of decay. But by day two, formerly bright blossoms will start to turn brown and shrivel, leaving you with a choice. You can allow the brown-edged blossoms to remain connected to the plant or you can take time to carefully pinch and remove the dying blossoms. If you ignore the decay and choose to allow the unhealthy blossoms to remain attached, your plant will soon be taken over by the decay. But if you choose to remove decaying flowers on a regular basis, then your plant will likely flourish.

DISCUSS THIS:
IF YOUR CONGREGATION WERE A PETUNIA, HOW MUCH AGREEMENT WOULD THERE BE IN THE CONGREGATION ABOUT WHICH PARTS OF YOUR MINISTRY OR MISSION ARE THE DYING BLOSSOMS THAT NEED TO BE REMOVED?

Farmers' Almanac offers clearer insights on why Jesus may have used the image of a grapevine. Pruning grapevines is essential because it ensures vines don't run rampant. More importantly, a grape cane (the shoot that holds the buds and grape clusters) can produce fruit one time. If a cane can produce fruit just once, a grape farmer must constantly be asking what must be pruned this year in order for fruit to grow next year. In fact, *Farmers' Almanac* suggests that a grape grower remove at least 90 percent of last season's growth since the more a farmer prunes, the more grapes will grow![2]

Imagine having to let go of 90 percent of what your congregation did this year in order to make room for next year's growth. Fortunately, congregations don't have to prune so significantly. But any healthy organization must let go of many things on a regular basis in order to see new fruit emerge.

The archives of many urban congregations paint a beautiful story of what has been. Boxes of records once recorded by the hundred-plus person choir are stacked away. Trophies won by church bowling, basketball, and softball leagues stand tall on top of the dust covering the file cabinets. Pictures of different Sunday school classes hang in frames. And Rolodexes still spin with the names of three thousand church members who were once sitting in the pews.

In some cases, the membership roster has not been audited in years, making it possible for a congregation to be oblivious to how much decline has taken place and impossible for its leaders to set goals based on a percentage of active members. More choir robes hang in a closet than are placed on bodies on any given Sunday, but the Director of Music remains a full-time position. And "ministries" that once made a difference in the lives of dozens of people are still being listed on the church calendar even though a new person has not participated in years. Meanwhile, the church's endowment, if there is one, is shrinking at an unsustainable pace.

Every congregation is faced with a choice. A congregation can choose to live or choose to decline and eventually die. If a congregation chooses life, the pruning shears are the first tool that must be taken out of the box.

But where do you start?

EXAMINING YOUR CURRENT SITUATION

The Bible is filled with images of fruit, and grapes are not the only fruit from which we can learn. A university extension office provides guidance on what to do if you move into a house that has old fruit trees. Trees that are dying or showing signs of decay can be restored through a judicious pruning process. But before doing whatever it takes to save the tree, the owner of the property should ask a series of questions.

"Is the tree worth saving? Did it formerly bear unique fruit that was exceptionally good for fresh eating or canning? Is the tree structurally sound—do the trunk and main limbs seem capable of bearing a heavy load of fruit, or would they simply break when heavily laden? Is the tree in a suitable location or does it shade the garden or interfere with lawn mowing?"[3]

What if we were to lead our congregations through a similar series of questions?

Is the church worth saving? Where is the church building located? Is the community around the facility growing, stable, or in decline? How many people live close enough to be able to walk to worship? Is there enough of a foundation remaining upon which to build? Are there committed leaders who are willing to let go in order to see what God might do in the future? While there are some congregations that need to let go altogether, there are countless other congregations that are ready to experience new life.

It's nearly impossible to go to a church leadership seminar without being asked to ponder the question, "Who would notice if your church no longer existed?" You may be in a place where no one would notice the church's closure with the exception of the people who are members of your church or worship there

7

regularly. If this is the case, then you may want to imagine who you would want to depend on your church in such a way that a penetrating void would be felt if you were to close. Can your church make a difference in the lives of these individuals? How will you start making a difference?

DISCUSS THIS:
WHO WOULD NOTICE IF YOUR CHURCH NO LONGER EXISTED? WHAT MINISTRIES OF YOUR CHURCH DOES THE COMMUNITY COUNT ON? WHICH ONES WOULD FEW PEOPLE MISS?

What are we willing to prune for new growth to occur? If you and your congregation believe you can take everything with you into God's intended future, then you may want to stop right now and simply hold on until there is nothing left to hold. But if you can imagine fully releasing certain habits, practices, ministries, and paid staff, then God may be ready to use you in abundant ways.

TRY THIS:
LIST EVERYTHING YOUR CONGREGATION DOES—EVERYTHING— AND THEN ASK: WHICH OF THESE THINGS ARE AT THE HEART OF WHO WE ARE, AND WHICH ARE PERIPHERAL?

Countless urban congregations are poised to experience new life—no matter how close they may be to death. In many places, the time has never been better for such change and transformation to happen as an increased demand for city living is escalating the construction of condominiums and apartments in the urban core of cities across our nation from Seattle to New York and Dallas to Minneapolis. Church buildings that were once surrounded by surface parking lots are now in the middle or on the edge of actual neighborhoods with runners, dog-walkers, and kids in strollers passing by at all hours of the day. And it's not just new people moving into the neighborhood. Even if the community around your church isn't experiencing this development, there are still people there, though they are often overlooked by churches seeking to grow—the so-called urban poor, individuals who are currently experiencing homelessness, and other people existing at the margins. Are you ready for your congregation to be just as vibrant as the community around you and become a part of that community's revitalization?

WHERE DO WE BEGIN?

The first step is to develop and strengthen relationships between the pastor and the members of the congregation. When Amy Butler became the senior pastor of the Riverside Church in New York City, she was given a congregation eager to move into God's intended future. Butler was aware that the congregation would first have to let go of some ministries and staff positions in order to grow again. She also knew these changes would be painful and require a significant amount of trust from the congregation. Butler sought to build relationships and credibility with her congregation through hosting "The Pastor's Table." Ten members were invited to come to Butler's home for breakfast or dinner. The listening sessions were designed to provide space for the congregation to get to know their new pastor while learning each other's hopes and dreams. Butler reflects on the experience of hosting these meals twice a month, noting that someone had been moved to tears at each gathering. She also watched as individuals who had been members of the same congregation for more than thirty years were just meeting each other, and people immediately commented on how grateful they were to know each other as well as their new pastor.

With relationships built, Butler was ready to start discerning what needed to be trimmed. She and her staff quickly realized there were duplicates of nearly everything. For example, a total of nine different groups within the congregation were doing prison ministry. She and her staff started to break down the silos and move people together. During one of the conversations, a staff member commented, "We have the equivalent of twenty-five Riversides but we just need one Riverside." It is this statement that formed the church's new branding of One Riverside, but it's also what helped them realign ministry to be more effective. However, Butler could have never led these changes without earning credibility first.[4]

DISCUSS THIS:
WHERE WITHIN YOUR CONGREGATION ARE EFFORTS BEING DUPLICATED? WHERE ARE YOU DUPLICATING MINISTRIES ELSEWHERE IN THE COMMUNITY?

CREATING A SENSE OF URGENCY

According to John P. Kotter, leading change requires creating a sense of urgency, and he offers nine ways to raise the urgency level in an organization. While we will take issue with Kotter's account of visionary leadership in chapter 2, his wisdom about creating urgency is essential for pastors and leaders ready for change. Two of the ways offered by Kotter are particularly helpful to urban congregations that are poised to grow and want to grow again: obvious examples of excess must be eliminated, and people must be bombarded with information on what can happen in the future and why the organization is currently unable to pursue those opportunities.[5]

Corporate examples of excess could include country-club memberships, gourmet dining rooms, and private jets—luxuries that are far from the scope and reality of any congregation. But there is plenty of excess in many of our churches. Some congregations have staff members who are no longer needed as the demand for different ministries or activities has diminished, making the keeping of a staff member a ministry in and of itself. Other congregations have not let go of a single ministry in decades, making today's calendar of activities comparable to the one that appeared on the back of a bulletin ten, twenty, or even forty years ago. We practice insanity well when we do the same thing over and over again while expecting different results.

Congregations are all too often stuck in the dreams of the past, allowing images of overflowing sanctuaries to cloud our view of today's painful reality of emptiness. The images of the past we cling to have a tendency to steer us wrong in discerning what is needed as we often see the church that was instead of the church that is. The church must learn to let go of the past and then both see and embrace its current circumstances in a way that allows it to look toward the future.

St. John of the Cross offered a powerful interpretation of God's desire to free us from our attachments and our nostalgic dreams in order to be more united in love with God. If we use his metaphor of the dark night of the soul and apply it to where the church is today, perhaps we can better see how God is seeking to free us from our current loves in order to embrace our one true love.

Many congregations have developed a burning passion for their church building. An image of the historic church building might be printed on every bulletin cover, business card, or sheet of stationery. Too often we define the church by the building, even if the building is in decay. The more monumental or historic the church building is, the more people are likely to see it as an object of affection and worship, even more than a living savior who gathers us inside to worship him. While many children learn to sing the words, "I am the church, you are the church, we are the church together," countless adults have convinced themselves that it is the building that matters, the building that beckons people in, the building that must be preserved.

TRY THIS:
ON A LARGE SHEET OF PAPER, WRITE "ASSET" AND "HINDRANCE" AT THE TOP, THEN BRAINSTORM WAYS YOUR CHURCH BUILDING IS AN ASSET TO VITAL MINISTRY, AND WAYS IT GETS IN THE WAY.

It took a booming commercial real estate market and an opportunity to sell property at the height of this market to break open the possibility of Mount Vernon Place detaching from the structure. But the possibility was as confusing and alarming as it was lucrative. How could a church be the church without a building? How could the church survive without the Chinese Community Church that had brought eighty to one hundred additional people to the main service each Sunday? How could the congregation let go of a chapel named for a beloved minister of music who labored for forty years in their midst?

The congregation literally had to move out of the building and let go of nostalgic dreams of the past in order to make space for God to first bring detachment and then visions of what could be. It was not long after moving day when the congregation started to learn how much they loved the building and all its contents for their sake instead of for Christ's sake. We loved more than fifteen pianos even though we only had a need for two. We loved silver tea sets even though they had not been used for forty years. We loved our stuff enough to even fight over it at a garage sale when neighbors finally stepped inside the building. The stuff made people feel good, bringing back memories of the past. But our stuff will never have the power to touch, change, and transform lives.

"Everything you love for its own sake, outside of God alone, blinds your intellect and destroys your judgment of moral values. It vitiates your choices so that you cannot clearly distinguish good from evil and you do not truly know God's will," wrote Thomas Merton with the kind of clarity and urgency that is needed today.[6]

Brave congregations that are ready to let go and plunge forward with God might find the following questions challenging and helpful to work through:

- How much of our church building and its contents do we love for our sake instead of for God's sake?

- How much of what we do in and for the church is for our own sake instead of for God's sake?

- What traditions do we love that have everything to do with our personal preferences or hard work and nothing to do with Jesus's efforts to change and transform the world?

- What are we doing or loving that we need to stop doing and loving?

- How much money are we spending to make one disciple of Jesus Christ?

- What would we do if we were working for Christ's sake alone?

ONGOING MINISTRY EVALUATION

Edgehill United Methodist Church is located a few blocks east of Vanderbilt University and Music Row in Nashville, Tennessee. The building is across the street from one of the largest public housing complexes in the city and in the middle of a neighborhood that was once overlooked but is now rapidly gentrifying. Residents of the neighborhood have created a community organizing non-profit called ONE (Organized Neighbors of Edgehill) "to improve the quality of life for all of the diverse people" in the community while seeking "to serve as a model and resource for other communities striving to stay economically and racially diverse by ensuring Edgehill remains a place we can ALL call home."[7] Edgehill UMC is a member of ONE with a long history of playing a vital role in the community.

The mission of Edgehill UMC as stated on their website is "to reach out to and welcome all persons as they are, in the name of Jesus Christ; to nurture one another in our relationship to God and in the Christian faith and life; [and] to go out as agents of God's transforming love to make our neighborhood and the world a place of justice and compassion."[8]

One can then quickly note how there are more ministries listed under "Community Outreach" than any other ministry heading. An emergency winter shelter, the ONE association, neighborhood scholarships, a community garden, a ministry to the elderly in the community, a restoration ministry, and another neighborhood partnership are all listed as ministries in which the congregation is engaged.

What you will not find listed anywhere on the website is a small group of church members known as the Ministry Evaluation Committee. This committee is charged with the task of determining if the church's ministries are effective. The committee regularly examines all that is being done by the congregation to see what may need to be refocused or laid to rest.

A recent member of the committee shared her experience of evaluating the church's longtime ministry with pregnant teenagers in the community. While the ministry had played a vital role in the lives of many individuals in the past, its reach had dwindled to one person being helped. The Ministry Evaluation Committee spent significant time looking at all the ministry had accomplished in the past, researched similar services available to the community, invited the community to evaluate the ministry, interviewed young teenage girls in the neighborhood to see where they were turning for help, and asked what they really needed and wanted. At the end of the evaluation period, it was determined that the particular ministry was no longer meeting a real need or playing the role it once played. The committee formed a plan to put the ministry to rest and worked with the pastor to determine how the ministry and its leaders who birthed it and led it could be recognized and celebrated in worship.

Imagine what might happen if there was a regular evaluation tool being used in our congregations to determine what was still effective and what had become ineffective, what was still making a vital difference and what was serving a handful of people, including its leaders. Imagine if we regularly embodied faithful pruning by celebrating what had been done in the past and looking for new ways of being even more faithful in the future.

FINDING YOUR FOCUS

Many people embrace the springtime to clean out closets, separating items that have not been worn or used in the last year. What if congregations were to embrace the same practice? What if a yard sale became an annual event where the congregation actually sold everything that is no longer being used, with all proceeds being invested in the wider community? The pruning could then continue outside of closets and classrooms as any small group, activity, or ministry that has not brought a newcomer or transformed a life in some real way in the previous twelve months is intentionally placed aside for a season.

A full calendar doesn't mean anything is actually happening. While businesses are regularly forced to evaluate which products are selling and which products remain on the shelf, churches are rarely forced to review which of their ministries are bringing new people through the doors, let alone have metrics to discern what ministries are touching and transforming lives. But imagine what could happen if we regularly committed to let go of anything that is no longer producing fruit? Furthermore, what if Jesus is expecting this action from us just as he expected it from his first disciples?

In his Farewell Discourse, Jesus makes it clear that people who are part of his community should expect to be pruned. It is the only way his community and movement will be sustained, let alone grow. Emily Askew explains, "Pruning involves taking off not only dead, lifeless branches but also those stems that still have life but that may nevertheless inhibit the overall strength and production of the larger vine."[9]

It's easier to identify the lifeless branches than it is the stems that are inhibiting our growth as a congregation. Where are clergy and lay leaders investing their time and attention? What is yielding fruit and what is draining resources, both spiritual and material? If you are a pastor, what two things could you stop doing today without many people noticing? What could you stop doing in the next year that fewer than ten people inside your church would even miss? What would you have to stop doing for anyone outside your church to notice?

In 2015, McDonald's announced that it was closing more stores than it would open that year—a decision that had not been made by the corporation in more than forty years. A *Washington Post* reporter was quick to criticize the fast food giant, pointing out the mistakes that led to the restaurant chain's decline: "McDonald's missteps are well-known. At a time when specialization is increasingly important in the food business, the brand has opted for breadth, offering everything under the moon:

hamburgers, salads, yogurt parfaits, and fancy chicken wraps. And it hasn't worked. In fact, that's putting it mildly."[10]

How often have our congregations offered the same amount of breadth, doing things it is no longer good at doing, offering programs that no one is continuing to choose? Where have we tried to add fancy chicken wraps instead of sticking with burgers and fries? What is no longer selling that we refuse to remove from our menu, allowing it to take up space in our refrigerator and freezer? McDonald's has learned that it must close fifty-nine more restaurants in one year than it is opening. How can we get back to doing only the things we do well?

The pruning shears are in your hands. What branches must be cut? What are you willing to let go of as you move into God's intended future?

TRY THIS:
TAKE THE LIST OF EVERYTHING YOUR CHURCH DOES AND PUT A STAR BY EACH ACTIVITY YOU CANNOT IMAGINE LETTING GO OF, AND THEN ASK WHY. IS IT BECAUSE THESE ACTIVITIES ARE MAKING A DIFFERENCE IN PEOPLE'S LIVES OR BECAUSE OF INERTIA?

Chapter Two

DESTINATION OR JOURNEY? RETHINKING VISION

THE TROUBLE WITH VISION

I n 2008, when Ginger and I (Roger) received our appointments to copastor Duke Memorial United Methodist Church in Durham, North Carolina, we felt pressure to succeed at renewing the church. The appointment was, to use leadership lingo, a "turnaround."

The founders of Duke Memorial in 1886 said the city needed a "mission chapel" to serve Durham's growing population.[1] By 1960, that new church was one of the largest churches in the conference, with six hundred people packing the beautiful sanctuary each Sunday morning.

By 2008, people were wondering where the masses had gone. The population of Durham had nearly tripled since 1960, but worship attendance at the church had declined by 60 percent. Several years of budget shortfalls and dipping into the endowment to make ends meet had disheartened leaders. One of the reasons two young, relatively inexperienced pastors were appointed to share one position was that the senior pastor's salary was cut by $20,000. The church could no longer afford the pastors they'd been used to.

"Do your best," one district superintendent told us. "But if you can't turn the church around, don't feel bad. The inertia of decline may be too strong."

The prevailing wisdom was clear about the kind of leader churches need, especially churches in this situation: they need visionary leaders. We heard this from every sector of the church—from judicatory leaders, from the most popular books, and from the Seven Habits of Highly Effective People seminar the conference paid for us to attend, where we learned that effective leaders "begin with the end in mind." In other words, they have a clear vision for where they are heading.

At that time, church leaders were looking to Bill Hybels of Willow Creek to discover the secrets of leading churches to grow. In his book *Courageous Leadership* he says that the leader's secret weapon is the power of vision. The leader is the one who "sees the vision"—one that makes his "pulse quicken"—and when he shares it, people can see the future, where the church is going, and they passionately get on board. Hybels writes that he hosts a vision night each year in his church where he casts the vision. He communicates it as clearly as possible so everyone understands exactly where they are going in order to provide impetus and focus for action.[2]

Hybels might have learned his account of vision from the classic and still popular view of visionary leadership provided by John Kotter, a retired professor from Harvard Business School. Kotter wrote an article called "What Leaders Really Do," in which he distinguished leadership from management. According to Kotter, this is what leaders really do:

- Leaders cast vision. They provide an organization with a clear picture of where the organization is headed.

- They set strategy. The organization needs to know how to get from here, where it is now, to there, the vision of the future. Strategy is the "how."

- They align systems. Leaders get all the parts, pieces, and people of an organization moving in the same direction.

- They communicate the vision. If people don't see it and remember it, they won't know where to go.

- Finally, leaders inspire broad-based action.[3]

I had read all the books. I felt I had to do what Kotter said to do. I wanted to cast clear, compelling vision like Bill Hybels. I'd read *Leadership Challenge* and knew a clear vision for the future was essential.[4] And I remember reading a book by a pastor who went on a retreat, heard God tell him the three-point vision for his church, and returned to offer the vision to the congregation.

We've heard again and again that without a vision the people perish (Prov 29:18). And leaders have the job of discovering and sharing that vision of the future.

Churches, we often imagine, need a Steve Jobs—cool pastors who stand on stage in their sleek black shirts and dazzle congregations with the picture of where the congregation can be in two, five, ten years. Simple, clear, compelling.

While I tried this and had some success, I began to have doubts. First, I began to worry that this model seemed too leader-centric. I felt stressed under the pressure of being the *one whose job it was to show the future*. But can one person have that job? And is that what a church needs from its pastors?

But that wasn't the only thing that bothered me.

IT'S THE CHARACTER OF THE JOURNEY

I began to believe this kind of visionary leadership promised a silver bullet to a problem that doesn't have any silver-bullet solutions. The disestablishment of the church in western culture, the rapidly and continuously changing culture in which churches find themselves, and the sense of fear, confusion, and malaise in so many churches cannot be fixed by an expert visionary who swoops in, casts vision, and inspires change. To use the popular language given us by Ron Heifetz and Marty Linsky, offering a clear vision of the future is a technical solution to an adaptive problem.[5] The problem is that in our rapidly changing world it's impossible to predict the future, to point on an unchanging map to our sure destination. The map is ever-changing, and what got us to our destination in former times doesn't work anymore.

Perhaps there are contexts where such a clear, compelling vision is just what is needed. And I'm sure there are leaders gifted to offer them. We are not saying that this kind of vision-casting is wrong. But our experience is that declining urban congregations that remember wistfully the days of the masses—days that are no more—are not those contexts. A stable vision, a clear picture of a destination that you can print on a postcard and memorize, is not adequate for the complex situations of declining urban congregations and the diverse and sometimes difficult contexts in which they find themselves.

Consider the elements that make many urban contexts unique, the characteristics of the contexts in which these churches find themselves.

- Multiculturalism. Cities have always been multicultural places, and are increasingly so. People from all backgrounds, countries, ethnicities, and religions populate our urban centers. Churches that are used to being homogenous need to adapt to this reality.

- Changing neighborhoods. Many urban congregations have been slow to recognize and respond to the reality that their neighbors aren't the same as they were fifty years ago. Often the core members of the church drive to the church building from the suburbs (if they haven't moved to a closer church) from their homogenous neighborhoods to their homogenous church that sits in the midst of a changing demographic.

- Socioeconomic disparity. As cities attempt to foster their own revitalization, the "urban poor" live in close proximity to spaces known for their "gentrification." People with low incomes fear that new housing, retail, and change in their neighborhoods will push them out.

- Racial conflict. The last few years and the Black Lives Matter movement made it abundantly clear that this country's conflicted racial past is far from over. Our cities are the places where these protests and movements have found a foothold, highlighting ongoing racial inequality, discrimination, and bias.

- Disestablishment. Furthermore, churches that once towered over cities as symbols of their power and importance have lost their prestige. Churches must adapt to and address all these changes while at the same time doing the work of rediscovering their own sense of identity when the identity given us by the culture has been stripped away.

DISCUSS THIS:
HOW DOES YOUR CONGREGATION EXPERIENCE EACH OF THESE CHARACTERISTICS? WHICH SEEM MOST RELEVANT TO YOUR CONGREGATION'S SITUATION OR CONTEXT?

The challenge for visionary leadership can be summed up in the difference between two kinds of change: continuous change and discontinuous change. Continuous change refers to change that is stable and predictable; the kind of change we are used to. In settings of continuous change, the vision-casting described above works beautifully. We can have a basic sense of how things will be different in a few years, and we can describe a future vision—our destination—accordingly.

Discontinuous change, on the other hand, is rapid and unpredictable. The speed and pace of technological innovation, for instance, is an example of discontinuous change. Industries dependent on technology struggle to predict what the lay of the land will be in just two or three years; no one knows how a new innovation will upend current practices and expectations. Discontinuous change is unpredictable. And in unpredictable settings we can't rely on a predictable destination.

In this urban church context, visionary leadership often leads to three mistakes.

First, the vision of the future too often looks like a vision of the past. We look backward to remember a time of flourishing, then we airbrush that picture a little bit and call it a vision of the future.

Second, the vision of the future looks just like what another church is doing. Instead of grappling with the change and variability where we are, we adopt someone else's vision, along with their proven plan to make the vision reality.

Third, the vision has a potential to be too specific and too narrow. "In five years, our worship attendance will have increased by 40 percent, and our number of small groups will have doubled." Unable to deal with the complexity of our contexts, we settle for narrow visions or wild guesses.

City churches are facing adaptive challenges. While a sense of where they are heading might help, what they need to learn are new ways of being—new habits, practices, and postures that keep them faithful, nimble, and responsive in the midst of often overwhelming change.

WHAT WE NEED INSTEAD— VISION AS THEOLOGICAL LANDSCAPE

John Kotter says in his classic book *Leading Change* that an organization needs a clear vision with specific measurable outcomes that can be articulated in a short paragraph.[6] I discovered that this kind of vision wasn't sufficient for the needs of the church in its context.

Fortunately, I encountered a gift. In the two years before my appointment, the church undertook a broad-based reevaluation of its mission and vision. A large percentage of the members of the congregation participated. The focus was more on discerning identity than prescribing narrow outcomes. And the result was a mission and vision statement broad enough and flexible enough for an urban church in a changing context. The vision statement clearly stated that the church intended to be a "sign and foretaste of God's kingdom in downtown Durham." That invitation didn't point to a clear destination in ten years; rather, it provided a landscape in which they hoped to live their life together—the landscape of God's kingdom. My wife, the leaders of the church, and I discovered that we needed such a vision, one that offered a wider context. Think of vision as painting the kingdom landscape in which the church seeks to live.

Mainline churches tend to use language of God's kingdom as a way to avoid embarrassment about Jesus. The discovery that the preaching of Jesus consisted of announcing God's kingdom gave us a way to look to something other than Jesus himself; his "kingdom" language could represent universal truths with which we all agree—justice, equality, and kindness. We didn't have to get more specific than that.

The theological vision that contributed to Duke Memorial's renewal, however, involved pointing again and again to the comforting, infuriating, and perplexing life and message of Jesus himself—the one who embodies God's kingdom, in his very person. If we are to be a sign of God's kingdom, then we can't ever stop exploring the landscape that is Jesus Christ, whose own life and mission is God's kingdom among us. Only within that landscape will we find our own particular vocation, our own unique vision.

And that unique vision will look less like a destination, and more like an account of how we will "be" on the journey of exploration.

When we imagine ourselves living as explorers on the landscape of God's kingdom, letting that landscape shape our life together and our witness in the world, we can find the same passion and inspiration that the vision gurus say a clear vision offers. Except we are not on a trip, making our way to a predictable destination; we are on an adventure. The destination is unknown, but the joy and the power and the fruit will come with how we live along the way.

TRY THIS:
BRAINSTORM AND LIST WHAT YOU TAKE TO BE THE CENTRAL CHARACTERISTICS OF GOD'S KINGDOM, THEN DISCUSS HOW YOUR CONGREGATION IS EMBODYING AND WITNESSING TO THESE CHARACTERISTICS.

Here's another way to put the difference: The old account of vision says we need to know *exactly where we are headed* before we start the journey; this account says we need a vision of the *kind of people we will be* on the journey, which will in large part determine where we end up.

There are advantages of thinking of vision as more of a landscape inhabited than a destination where one arrives, advantages that relate well to the adaptive challenges facing urban congregations. Vision-as-theological landscape:

- Makes room for *improvisation*. When the future is unpredictable, we must be able to improvise. But how do we know what a faithful improvisation looks like—a new ministry, for instance, or a change in worship? We ask: Does it fit within the landscape as we are coming to understand it? Jesus improvised. When he fed the five thousand he was confronted with an unexpected situation: It was late and the people were hungry. So he decided to feed them; he improvised. Take what little we have, share it, and in the power of God discover that it's more than enough (Matt 14:13-21).

- Allows for *flexibility and agility*. As with improvisation, we must be flexible, agile, and able to respond to the unexpected. Organizations with a rigidly defined vision struggle to do this. But when you see your vision as faithfully inhabiting a kingdom landscape, always looking to Jesus, then you can take a detour and be okay. Jesus did that. On his way to heal the slave of an important official, Jesus discovered that a woman who had been hemorrhaging for years tugged on his garment. Rather than press on to his defined destination, he was flexible enough to heal this person waiting on his path (Matt 9:18-22).

- Provides space for *experimentation*. If we don't know exactly where we are going, we need spaces in congregations to experiment and try new things. Some have called these spaces emergent zones. Vision-as-landscape allows for shaping a culture of experimentation, of trial and error (see chapter 3 for more on this).

- Allows for a *permission-giving culture*. Bill Easum writes about how congregations need to have a "permission-giving" culture.[7] By this he means as we come to a clearer sense of our identity, and know the kingdom-landscape in which we seek to live and minister, we can better say "yes" to people with new ideas. All the ideas, all the vision, doesn't need to come from the top. When members of a congregation see a narrow, destination-style landscape, they can feel paralyzed, uncertain how they can contribute. But when a vision is a theological landscape of God's kingdom that points us again and again to Jesus, then many can have their imaginations inspired and find ways they can contribute.

- Requires *ongoing discernment*. Most importantly, if our vision is a landscape of God's kingdom, then the vision invites us to discern in an ongoing way how best we can respond to the presence of God who brings the kingdom in the world and in our midst. Vision-as-destination doesn't ask this kind of discernment; you already know where you are going.

DISCUSS THIS:
WHAT KIND OF VISION DOES YOUR CHURCH HAVE—NARROW AND SPECIFIC OR WIDE AND ROOMY? WHICH OF THESE CHARACTERISTICS DOES YOUR VISION ALLOW?

SO WHAT DOES THE LEADER DO?

So what does a pastor do if she doesn't cast the vision and describe the destination in vivid detail to the congregation?

First, we'll tell you what she doesn't do: corner every parishioner at every moment and give a "stump speech" about where the church needs to go. One author has suggested that any conversation a pastor has with a parishioner that doesn't cast vision for where the congregation needs to go is missing key opportunities, and that every pastoral interaction is a chance to cast vision, to offer a clear picture of where the congregation is going; to make converts to the pastor's vision. "Think of yourself as a persuader. A good stump speech is trying to make converts even out of those who think they are with you.... People and their finances are attracted to those who believe that they are going to make a difference."[8]

There's certainly nothing wrong with being energetic and inspiring when we talk about the future. But churches will be more faithful—and many pastors will be less stressed—when pastors lay down the mantle of persuader-in-chief and recover their proper work as pastoral leaders and become theologians again and spiritual guides, helping congregations discern the most faithful way to live in the kingdom landscape.

That proper work means more than giving vision stump speeches and being a persuader. The leader gets to have more fun as she recovers her role as *interpreter, storyteller, imagination inspirer,* and *discernment facilitator.*

The pastor as *interpreter* performs the ongoing task of interpreting God's kingdom here and now. She spends time in the scriptures and in prayer, trying to understand how the ancient language of God's reign inaugurated in Christ and witnessed to by the church helps us to see more clearly our identity and purpose here and now. The mission statement at Duke Memorial when I arrived said that the church wanted to be a "sign and foretaste of God's kingdom in downtown Durham." But what does that mean? Week in and week out, through sermons and Bible studies and devotions before meetings, the pastor gets to help interpret the reality of God's kingdom for us here and now.

The pastor helping to lead a church in renewal also becomes a *storyteller.* He will look for and tell stories of how the church is already embodying its identity and purpose in God's kingdom. Where are signs of faithfulness as we inhabit together the landscape of God's kingdom? Where is fruit beginning to grow on the newly pruned branches? Where are shoots of new life already visible? For many churches struggling to live into a future full of hope, despair blinds the eyes to these signs of life and faithfulness. The leader then acts as a mirror—showing the church's life to itself, helping it see both the times when it simply wants to bury its head, but also where it is responding faithfully to God's always in-breaking kingdom.

I (Roger) heard Donna do this once in a particularly memorable sermon. The church had discerned that one of the ways it was being called to inhabit the landscape of God's kingdom in its particular context was to practice hospitality throughout its life and work. It is not "casting a vision" in the traditional sense when Donna says, "As we continue to grow in faith as a congregation, I've learned that there are two things most important to us as a body. One is being a church where all are abundantly welcome. The other is providing a way to be a blessing to people who are currently unhoused." She's not *telling* the congregation where it needs to go or what it will look like in five years. Rather, she's reflecting back to the congregation the very heart of its life in God's kingdom that they discerned together. Much of the rest of the sermon tells stories about where she has seen this kind of hospitality happening in the congregation.

TRY THIS:
BY YOURSELF OR (PREFERABLY) AS A GROUP, THINK OF THREE STORIES THAT SHOW HOW YOUR CHURCH IS EMBODYING GOD'S KINGDOM RIGHT NOW, THEN DECIDE HOW YOU WILL TELL THESE STORIES TO THE WIDER CONGREGATION.

Along with interpreting God's kingdom here and now and pointing to ways the congregation is already living in that kingdom, the pastor *inspires the imagination*. No one can see the future with certainty; so we are unable to say, especially amidst constant change, exactly where we will be and what we will be doing. But that doesn't mean we can't inspire the imagination and help people to ask: If we continue to live our identity in God's kingdom with increasing faithfulness, what can we imagine we might see happen? What might our fruit begin to look like?

This is exactly what Donna did in that sermon. She reflected to the congregation its own commitment to hospitality, told stories about where that hospitality is already being embodied, and then asked what might be next. Where are the places and the ways this hospitality can be extended? She offered examples from her own praying and imagining: "This week I've allowed myself to dream. I've been dreaming a lot, and my mind and heart have been consumed with what we could do." And then she shared her dreams—not to make "converts" to her side, and not to impose a vision untested by prayer and the congregation's discernment, but to inspire their own holy imagining. Her dreams weren't an agenda for the church she planned to push. Rather, they were examples of what the congregation could be if it continued to follow Jesus faithfully through the landscape of God's kingdom.

Finally, the pastor acts as *facilitator of discernment.* Given our growing understanding of the kingdom, our sense of how we are already faithfully living in its landscape, and imaginations opened and awakened to holy possibilities, we finally get to the question: What do we do next? The traditional answer, imported along with vision-casting from the business world is: Come up with a strategic plan, one that will get you from point A to point B.

Certainly there is planning involved. But if renewal is more about living into God's kingdom than about what we want to do, then what urban congregations need, more than a strategic planner, is a discernment facilitator—someone who can create the spaces for the congregation to begin to ask and answer questions like: Given who we are, our unique identity in this time and place—in *this* city—what is God inviting us to do? What new ways are we being invited to embrace? The next chapter will address this more thoroughly. But first, an example of a "kingdom landscape" vision in one urban congregation.

AN EXAMPLE

A few miles from downtown Pittsburgh, on the border between the communities of Highland Park and East Liberty, close to some of Pittsburgh's struggling schools and aware of the redevelopment that is often called "regentrification" of East Liberty, lies Open Door Church, a ten-year-old Presbyterian congregation. As a young congregation, they aren't facing many of the challenges of old, declining congregations. But the rest of us can learn from the way they understand their identity and mission.

If you go to their website, you will be hard-pressed to find a typical vision statement. Under the "About Us" tab, however, you will find two tabs called "Community Practices" and "Values." And here is where you will see how they understand themselves. They don't see themselves as a community marching straightforwardly to a clearly defined destination. Rather, they have interpreted how they are being called to embody God's kingdom as a particular *kind* of community. This is less about *where they are headed* (vision in the traditional sense) and more about *how they will be as they journey together.*

So what do the people at Open Door value? Reverence, friendship, transformation, authenticity, being Spirit-led, rootedness, struggle, and innovation. As they have come to understand God's kingdom, they know that they value these aspects and seek to embody them in their common life.

Perhaps more important than a list of values is the category "Community Practices." This category takes the place of the more typical category of "Vision." Their common life is shaped by five cornerstone practices:

- Listen to God.

- Learn from God.

- Eat with Others.

- Encourage Others.

- Give Ourselves away to the World.[9]

"When I came to Open Door, I found this so refreshing." This is what we heard when we spoke to Margaret, a woman who is a member of the church and a leader. "I came to Open Door from a suburban church that went every year to the Willow Creek Leadership Summit. We tried to do what Bill Hybels told us to do about vision, but it wasn't working, wasn't helping us listen to God. What's most important is not where we are going to be in the end, but how God is leading us to the next step. We discover that through our core practices."

The church weaves these practices through all it does. In corporate worship they practice silence together in order to listen to God, learn from God through the scriptures, and eat with one another at Holy Communion each week. The weekly prayer following Communion reinforces their identity as a community living in God's kingdom through shared practices. Their new member process introduces new members to these core practices, which they commit themselves to when they take their membership vows. And as leaders, they try to be intentional about pointing out when they are "doing" together a practice, even when it might not be obvious. Margaret continued, "If you asked folks what our vision is— we don't really use that language though—they would talk about our core practices. They are narrow enough to be defined practices, but broad enough to allow flexibility and discovery. Our faithfulness to these practices helps us to see what the next step is.

DISCUSS THIS:
WHAT DOES YOUR CONGREGATION VALUE? WHAT ARE THE PRACTICES THAT GUIDE YOU? HOW ARE THOSE PRACTICES TAUGHT, ENCOURAGED, AND MODELED BY LEADERS?

"Our urban setting doesn't have the stability of my old church in the suburbs. When I moved to this neighborhood, we had three shootings in the same year. Things change, circumstances disrupt us. The most important thing is who we are and how we are going to journey faithfully together."

This is how they embody together God's kingdom, how they live in that landscape. And one of the values of this kind of vision is that it endures despite ongoing, rapid change. They are constantly discerning together how they will do these things and what the fruit will be. They trust that when they do these things, they will be receiving into their lives the ways of Jesus, and, on branches pruned of the unnecessary, kingdom fruit will flourish.

EYES WIDE OPEN: RETHINKING STRATEGY

DON'T WE NEED A STRATEGY?

I f we continue to view vision as the destination to be reached, then we need a plan, a detailed map that will ensure we get from here to there in a specified amount of time—right? And even if we consider that vision might not so much be a clearly defined destination as a landscape in which we are learning to live faithfully, our default, especially when things aren't going well (and for many city churches, things don't seem to be going well), is to put together a strategic plan. We are so accustomed to taking our marching orders from the *Harvard Business Review* that we don't know what else to do. Don't we need to make a strategic plan?

Yes.

And no.

We need something. But we don't necessarily need a traditional strategic plan: a list of goals and objectives, strategies, and tasks that promise to get us from here to there in the requisite months or years. The discussion in the previous chapter should help us see one reason we don't need such a plan: This kind of plan relies too much on predictability. But as we've seen, especially for churches in rapidly changing urban centers, accurate prediction is impossible. This kind of plan also assumes that we can decide what we need to do before we do anything; from the safe confines of a conference room we can determine goals, objectives, and strategies to achieve them, and then we press Go! and implement the plan. This, too, is a false assumption. More often, we discover what to do next by doing something now.

Our contemporary context requires that we be willing to act before we have all of the information; that we be willing to experiment in the absence of a clearly defined endpoint; that we be willing to learn along the way; that we keep our eyes open and be willing to discover the next, new faithful step as it emerges. And all of this means learning to be comfortable with uncertainty and ambiguity.

One way of putting our critique of traditional strategic planning is this: It implies what some have called "functional atheism." We in our churches can speak eloquently about God, as Parker Palmer said, but when we look at how we actually live together and perform our common work, we more often act like God is not involved. We assume that "if anything decent is going to happen here, we are the ones who must make it happen—a conviction held even by people who talk a good game about God."[1]

If we truly trust that God is at work in our complicated, ever-changing contexts, then we don't need to wait until we have the right strategic plan—the perfect map—before we begin to explore the landscape of God's kingdom and practice what our faithfulness will look like as we let the story of the kingdom shape our life together in the city.

Organizational theorist Karl Weick offers a parable that helps to show why it's a myth that we need the "right" strategic plan, or even that the right plan exists, especially in a system that is stuck (like a declining church in a changing culture):

> The young lieutenant of a small Hungarian detachment in the Alps sent a reconnaissance unit into the icy wilderness, it began to snow immediately, snowed for two days, and the unit did not return. The lieutenant suffered, fearing that he had dispatched his own people to death. But the third day the unit came back. Where had they been? How did they make their way? Yes, they said, we considered ourselves lost and waited for the end. And then one of us found a map in his pocket. That calmed us down. We pitched camp, lasted out the snowstorm, and then with the map we discovered our bearings. And here we are. The lieutenant borrowed this remarkable map and had a good look at it. He discovered to his astonishment that it was not a map of the Alps but a map of the Pyrenees.

Weick interprets this parable:

> This incident raises the intriguing possibility that when you are lost any old map will do. Extended to the issue of strategy, maybe when you are confused, any old strategic plan will do. Strategic plans are not like maps. They animate people and they orient people. Once people begin to act, they generate tangible outcomes in some context, and this helps them to discover what is occurring, what needs to be explained, and what should be done next.[2]

In other words, a strategic plan is not a map that will guarantee to get us to our destination, but a catalyst for learning, experimentation, and discovery. And since many of our urban congregations feel like they are lost in a snowstorm, this might be just the kind of strategy we need.

WHAT GOOD STRATEGIES DO

So, if good strategies don't provide a foolproof map to get us from point A to point B, what *do* good strategies do?

Here's where we need to think about the process of planning, rather than thinking of a strategic plan as a product. If the end product—the plan—is all that matters, then we will develop the plan in ways that obstruct any possibilities inherent in the plan itself by valuing efficiency over collaboration. Many churches have a drawer, perhaps in the pastor's desk, where unrealized strategic plans go to rest; or perhaps there is a niche in the church's columbarium where they put the ashes of old strategic plans whose potential never saw the light of day because the focus was on the plan itself and not on the process of the planning. Before turning to the next section and outlining the elements of a good planning process, let's pause and consider the values of good plans and the processes that created them.

FIRST, GOOD STRATEGIC PLANS AND PROCESSES OPEN US TO GOD.

I (Roger) was part of a strategic planning process for a Christian organization where I'm on the board. From the beginning I advocated that we take time in our strategic planning team meetings to do an examen at the end of each meeting, to ask questions like: Where did we sense God's presence leading us in this meeting? And where do we still need God to give us clarity, guidance, and courage? Taking time for silence, prayer, and conversation around these kinds of questions can allow a planning process to be a period of deep spiritual growth for a church or a community. Unfortunately, this organization decided on a generic prayer to be read at the beginning of each meeting and then to get on with business as usual.

The problem is this: As we suggested above, business as usual tends toward functional atheism—the mistaken belief that we are the initiators of anything good that's going to happen here. But the reality is just the opposite: God is already at work in this congregation, in the neighborhood surrounding the congregation, and in the culture whose rapid changes bring so much fear and consternation. What Eugene Peterson has said about pastoral ministry broadly is equally true of strategic planning: "When I engage in conversation, meet with a committee, or visit a home, I am coming in on something that has already been in process for a long time. God has been and is the central reality in that process. . . . My work is . . . to discover what [God] is doing and live appropriately with it."[3] We could rewrite that for our purposes: When we begin a process of planning, we do it trusting that this process will help us discover what *God* is doing in our midst and in the world, and respond appropriately. Good plans and the processes that create them do just that.

SECOND, GOOD PLANS OPEN US TO NEW ACTIONS.

At their heart, good plans give congregations the freedom to try something new, to overcome the two types of paralysis that afflict congregations facing momentous changes. The first is the paralysis caused by the despair of change and decline. The paralysis of resignation sets in when everything seems overwhelming, and there's nothing we could do that would make a difference. A good plan overcomes this by opening us to new actions, and small experiments free us from the weight of having to save the day. As in the parable above, the plan spurred the lost hikers to begin to take some steps, and that was all that was needed. When we begin to take some steps, having been part of a process that opens us to what God is doing in our midst and in the world, we can trust that the actions we take aren't last ditch efforts to right a sinking ship, but are faithful responses to what God is inviting us to do.

The second kind of paralysis is the paralysis caused by having to "get it right"—the paralysis of perfectionism. In chapter 5 on excellence, you will learn of our commitment to doing the best we can, to paying attention to detail in every aspect of a church's ministry. But sometimes, when a commitment to excellence becomes perfectionism, the result is paralysis: we don't do anything because we are afraid of getting it wrong. But recognizing in rapidly changing urban environments that no silver bullets can turn around a church—and that turning around shouldn't be the goal anyway—should free us from the fear that we might get it wrong. When we begin planning with this freedom in mind, we no longer need to suffer from either of these paralyses.

THIRD, GOOD PLANS OPEN OUR EYES TO NEW POSSIBILITIES.

Sometimes the process of planning or taking action on a plan helps us see what we *should have done* and correct course. I (Roger) used to tell my congregation: The reason we need a plan with points A, B, and C is that sometimes only when you get to point C, do you see what A should have been.

In 2005, Mount Vernon Place undertook a major effort to redevelop their property, which helped them to re-envision their building and ministry. As part of their process, they spent months dreaming about the needs of the congregation and the community. Knowing that youth groups from across the country visit the nation's capital and need lodging, they included plans for showers, so they could host these youth groups.

And it was these very plans that opened them to other possibilities of ministry. Only *after* the showers were installed were they able to fully see a more immediate need right in front of them. The same showers could be useful to the people living and sleeping on the church porticos and in the parks around downtown Washington. Thus began their shower ministry, which has become one of the most important ways the church is in ministry with its community.

And when folks who used the shower ministry began coming to worship, it opened the congregation's eyes to ways they could be even more hospitable. All because a plan to renovate the building helped them see new possibilities.

FINALLY, GOOD PLANS AND THEIR PROCESSES HELP US EXPERIENCE OUR CONGREGATIONS AS MYSTERIES TO BE INHABITED RATHER THAN PROBLEMS TO BE SOLVED.

Certainly, we can go into a planning process hoping this will solve the problem of decline; we can do it with that mindset. But a good planning process will train us out of seeing congregations as problems to be solved. When we go through a good planning process, we begin to see that there is more going on here than problems, that this church—however we are experiencing decline, however unsettling are the changes we are facing—this church is a deep mystery where God is present and at work and where God and humans are united. A good planning process can help us recover this vision—*if* we move away from a frantic search for technical fixes and rediscover our congregations and their neighborhoods as the playgrounds of God's life-giving Spirit.

DISCUSS THIS:
IN YOUR CONVERSATIONS ABOUT RENEWAL, DOES YOUR CONGREGATION TYPICALLY GET DESCRIBED MORE AS A PROBLEM OR AS A MYSTERY WHERE GOD IS AT WORK? WHY DO YOU THINK THIS IS THE CASE?

ELEMENTS OF A PLANNING PROCESS

What are the elements of a good planning process? We resist the temptations to offer a foolproof blueprint for successful planning—because we don't have one. No one does. Each congregation is different, and the planning needs differ. One congregation might be planning how to re-imagine adult Christian formation, while another might be planning a multimillion dollar building project.

But there are good planning processes, which can adapt to whatever situation the congregation is facing. Before we outline those elements, consider the most important word in the language of church planning: *discernment*. Discernment is a way of discovering who we are and what we should do that puts responding to God's initiative at the very center. Unlike much strategic planning, discernment is theocentric. It's focused on God. Graham Cray, a Church of England bishop leading their Fresh Expressions initiative, said recently in a conversation with some seminary professors that discernment is the number one capacity the church needs in leaders today. We would add: It's the most important capacity of congregations themselves.

DISCUSS THIS:
WHEN HAS YOUR CONGREGATION DISCERNED SOMETHING WELL? HOW WAS DISCERNMENT DIFFERENT FROM OTHER WAYS OF MAKING A DECISION?

Do we know how to discern what God is doing, and how should we participate? That is the most important question. The following elements of a discerning/planning process help a congregation do just that.

CLARITY ABOUT THE QUESTION

As we plan together—as we seek to discern faithful steps for a congregation living amidst urban change—we must begin with clarity about what we are discerning. In a helpful book on decision-making in the church, New Testament scholar Luke Timothy Johnson breaks questions of discernment into two broad categories: identity and task.[4] We find this a helpful distinction, even though we agree with Johnson that the "distinction is a loose one, with disputed borders."[5]

Many congregations in changing urban contexts are facing *identity* questions: Who are we? What is our purpose? Why are we here? In the era of Christendom (when everyone by birth was assumed to be Christian), these questions were seldom asked. But as our neighborhoods changed and the pews became empty, these questions surfaced. They are fundamental questions, questions a congregation needs to answer before it turns to other forms of planning.

But there are also *task* questions: What should we do? How should we change? These questions force us to talk about actions we want to take, actions we think God is leading us to take, actions we might be afraid to take. Having clarity about what we are discerning and planning is important to make the process go well.

DISCUSS THIS:
WHICH OF THESE—IDENTITY OR TASK—IS
YOUR CONGREGATION READY TO DISCERN?

Obviously, these areas are related. So often we don't know what to do because we don't know who we are or why we are here; we lack a sense of purpose, an identity. In that case, our planning around actions and tasks will be like frantically shooting arrows in the dark. They will arise out of our confusion and anxiety. But as we begin to discover a renewed sense of identity and mission in God's kingdom breaking into our cities, we will discover ourselves naturally asking task questions: If this is who we are, and this is what God seems to care about, then what should we *do*?[6]

DEEPER ACKNOWLEDGEMENT AND UNDERSTANDING
OF THE CURRENT REALITY

Any discernment process, especially one that involves planning ministry to facilitate change in the face of uncertainty and decline, needs to create space for members of the congregation to notice and name how they are experiencing their current situation. They need spaces where, without fear of judgment or being corrected, they can articulate the anxieties, fears, and hopes they have, many of which they have likely not been able to name. Alan Roxburgh and Fred Romanuk describe this need:

> For people in our congregations, the world is spinning. So much is happening, but they have little space to process their experience and give it meaning. They come to worship with many questions and feelings that never get addressed. People sense something is wrong with the state of Christian life but don't know how to express that feeling. They don't know how to articulate what lies beneath the diffuse anxiety and can't put words to the confusion.... Until people can put their feelings into words and be heard, they are held captive by unarticulated anxiety. Leaders must create a listening space to allow people to become aware of what is happening within and among them.[7]

People in congregations need to be given the freedom to name what they are experiencing in relationship to what is being planned or discerned, otherwise they will want to jump to quick fixes and technical solutions. For many urban congregations, the changes in our culture are unsettling; others see them as hopeful. Most often they are a mixture of both. Giving congregations space to name their experiences of disequilibrium is key to moving forward in faithful ways, not least because in these spaces where people are free to speak, the Holy Spirit is often heard among them.

GATHERING AND REVIEWING DATA AND OTHER INFORMATION

Having gained clarity around which issues a congregation is trying to discern and plan, and having been given the freedom that comes with expressing honestly hopes, fears, and anxieties, a congregation then needs opportunities for collecting data and other useful information, and the space to ask: Given what we are seeing in this information, what are we learning that is relevant to the decisions we have to make? Sometimes the information gathered helps a congregation see more clearly any incongruence between its vision and understanding of God's kingdom and its current ways of living as a community.[8]

At this point, it's important to think broadly about data and information gathering. We are tempted to look for that one piece of information that will bring understanding and also unlock the future. It doesn't exist. Many people think that easily obtainable demographic data is the key. Demographic reports can tell us about who lives near a church, how a neighborhood has changed, and what the preferences and predilections are of the kinds of people living in a neighborhood. Armed with this information, we begin to plan and market programs to people we have only learned about through a website. Demographic data is not enough.

Nothing can replace actually getting to *know* your neighbors, meeting the actual people, hearing their stories, and seeing how God is already at work in them. One of the values of this work is that we learn the people in our neighborhoods are not just people with needs to be ministered to but people with gifts and graces, imaginations, and skills whom we can be in ministry with. As we hear their stories and histories, their dreams and fears, we might begin to see more clearly where God's initiative is at work. This initiative can't be read off of a demographic printout.

TRY THIS:
BRAINSTORM EVERYTHING YOUR CONGREGATION WOULD NEED TO KNOW IN ORDER TO DISCERN AND PLAN WELL. NOW MAKE A PLAN TO BEGIN COLLECTING SOME OF THIS INFORMATION.

Faith United Methodist Church is a small congregation nestled in the Fox Chapel Borough outside of Pittsburgh, one of the wealthiest neighborhoods in Pennsylvania. It is by no means an urban congregation, but Fox Chapel is close to some boroughs that are nearer to the city, boroughs facing many of the more typical urban realities: poverty, drug abuse, racial tension, and struggling schools. The people of Faith UMC felt called to ministry in one of these boroughs called Sharpsburg, but they were not sure what they should do. Rather than researching the "problems" of the area, then imposing solutions, they decided they needed to get to know the people of Sharpsburg. First they simply took walks with their eyes wide open, then gathered after these walks to share what they were seeing, hearing, and feeling. This kind of on-the-ground information gathering told them much more than demographic data.

They discovered that they didn't know the area, even though many of their children went to the same schools. It was too soon to engage in ministry planning. Instead, they hosted a community dinner twice a month at the Senior Citizen Center with no agenda other than to create the space for people from two communities to get to know one another and hear one another's stories. This "data gathering" lasted more than a year before any other "tasks" were considered.

EXPLORATION AND REFINEMENT OF POSSIBILITIES

Eventually, a turn will be made. Ideas will begin to emerge. New possibilities can be explored. Typically, when a church in decline tries to solve problems—to fix the decline—it introduces what we've learned to call *technical solutions*, solutions they have tried before that worked at one time. But they don't work now. In fact, now we don't even know what it means for something to "work." But after a patient discernment process, in which we've agreed on the issue before us, spent considerable time sharing our hopes and anxieties, and gathered data and information broadly, we will discover that things we haven't tried—new, perhaps risky ideas—begin to emerge. This is the space for innovative thinking and imagining. This is not the time to say what's wrong with any idea—who knows at this stage what the "right" one is? In fact, Danny Morris and Charles Olson suggest that at this stage, the group needs to focus on making each idea the best that it can be. They call this the phase of "exploring" and "improving."[9]

At this stage, resist the urge to get it "right," or to rush. Hold loosely any idea that's offered. Allow the craziest ideas to be expressed. Free from the idea that we can find one silver bullet to solve our problems—indeed, freed from the idea that the church is a problem to be solved—we can explore previously unexplored ideas with less fear, even with some excitement.

TRY THIS:
LIST FIVE NEW POSSIBILITIES THAT MIGHT BE RIGHT FOR YOUR CONGREGATION. MAKE THEM AS GOOD AS YOU CAN. WHICH SEEM TO HAVE THE MOST ENERGY OR EXCITEMENT AROUND THEM? WHICH SEEM MOST IN LINE WITH THE CONGREGATION'S IDENTITY?

EXPERIMENTATION

The word *experiment* is liberating. Rather than thinking at this stage we need to make a decision or draft the definitive plan for the next five or ten years, we launch experiments. Knowing that it's difficult to predict how any one idea will pan out, and believing that in experimentation and innovation we can continue to discover how God is leading us, we experiment. We work to not have too much invested in any one option, but we take what begins to seem like the one or two best, and we try them and see what happens. For Faith UMC, hosting community meals was an experiment. No one knew that in three years two other churches would be involved, hundreds of new relationships would be made, free legal and medical clinics would be held, and community art shows would be sponsored.

DISCUSS THIS:
WHAT DIFFERENCE WOULD IT MAKE IN YOUR CONGREGATION TO THINK OF NEW VENTURES AS EXPERIMENTS? DOES IT MAKE IT EASIER TO TAKE RISKS?

ONGOING ASSESSMENT AND COMMITMENT

The information gathering and data collection doesn't stop. As we experiment with those ideas that emerged from our shared discernment and as we begin new efforts consistent with our growing understanding of God's kingdom, we continue to listen and learn. Which experiments seem to be gaining traction? Which seem to be blessed by God's Spirit? Which ones are falling flat, draining energy, causing burnout? By continuing to pay attention to these things, a congregation can then begin to see where they need to commit their time and energy in ministry, to which innovative efforts they need to continue to direct their attention. Furthermore, in the process of reviewing the experiments, other possibilities will emerge, and the congregation will discover itself in a virtuous cycle of innovation, experimentation, and commitment as it walks with God into renewal.[10]

Russ Moxley is a veteran consultant to organizations and leaders—from Fortune 500 companies to local congregations—and a former faculty member of the Center for Creative Leadership in Greensboro, North Carolina. He has helped countless organizations and congregations through the morass of planning, and he has come to a conclusion: Effective planning requires comfort with order and with chaos. He tells the story of a corporation he worked in that tried to plan out chaos; it was uncomfortable with the unexpected. Their planning process was completely linear. When unforeseen situations arose, they decided to plan more often rather than learning to incorporate the unforeseen in the plan they had. He says their planning process "was clean and neat and orderly. I liked it. It didn't work."[11] Now he knows that planning needs to be a "blending of intentional and emergent strategy."[12] "Intentional" refers to the necessary order of a planning process—the things we put in place, the goals and outcomes we hope to achieve. "Emergent" means that in any process of planning and executing there needs to be openness to chaos—the intentional letting go of control—so that unexpected actions can emerge, unanticipated obstacles can be addressed, and unforeseen opportunities can be grasped.

When a planning process in a church becomes a *discerning* process, it does exactly what Moxley says it should do: moves with intentionality *and* remains open to emergence. And in congregations, we commit to remaining open to what emerges, to planning and living with eyes wide open, because we know we follow a God who can't be managed or controlled and who won't be satisfied with our merely following a linear path to meet our objectives. When the elements above are creatively incorporated into any planning process, we can be confident intentionality and emergence will result in seeing and responding to God's own surprising ways.

SO WHAT DOES A LEADER DO?

It looks like we are robbing the leader of his or her job. First we said it's not the leader's job alone to cast the vision and set goals for the congregation; indeed, maybe the traditional way of understanding vision and goals are incongruent with what God needs from urban congregations in their new, changing missional contexts. Now we are suggesting that an orderly, linear plan—a process perhaps led by the senior pastor?—is not the way congregations need to plan for ministry if they want to remain available to see and respond to what God is doing in the church and in the world. So what is a leader to do? In the last chapter of the book we'll look more explicitly at leadership, arguing for a shared leadership approach. But still, there are pastors and lay leaders with positions of leadership, and the question remains: How can they help this blend of intentional and emergent planning to work?

First, and most importantly, the leaders can keep the process spiritually centered on God by inviting times of silence and reflection, insisting that in an ongoing way, throughout the process, those involved stop to ask where they are seeing God at work.

Another thing leaders can do is create the space for the process to happen and help the congregation understand the importance of a good planning process. As the church looks at different mod els of planning and discernment, or as it thinks about bringing in a consultant to help, the leaders can make clear the commitment to a process with the elements above that makes the space for listening to and responding to God. This means the leader will exhibit patience, and patience is contagious. When leaders show patience with an open process, and advocate one that doesn't tie up all the loose ends, this patience will subtly shift a culture of impatience that wants solutions and wants them now.

Also significant, leaders are in the position many times to begin to name the issue that needs to be addressed or identify an area around which discernment and planning need to happen and then invite others into the process. Peter Block calls this "leadership as convening," and it's an underappreciated aspect of leadership.[13] Leaders can call people together; set the stage for a theocentric, open process; and suggest areas that need attention, even if the exact question or issue needs to be refined by the group. This book suggests several areas for which urban congregations might need to discern. A leader can direct attention to one or more of them and initiate a process.

Leaders also need to speak into this process authentically, openly, and respectfully. They need to say, "Here's what I'm seeing. Here's what I'm thinking. Here's what we might need to do, from my perspective," knowing that theirs is not the only voice in the conversation. One of the most common critiques of leadership-as-convening-discerning-conversations is: What about when the leader has a vision to share? The answer to this objection is: Share it. When members of the congregation, co-leaders, and participants in a discerning/planning process know that the leader is authentic and has integrity and isn't orchestrating a process to push through a predetermined agenda, then folks will listen to the ideas, concerns, and visions of a leader, and give them the weight and respect they deserve.

Leaders can also say "yes" more often. When a congregation has a clear understanding of its vision—that is, its way of being in the world consistent with the priorities of God's kingdom and unique to its own character and context—and when it is trying to embrace a culture of discernment and experimentation, the leaders of a congregation (pastors, committee chairs, people with power but with no particular position) need to learn to say "yes" to ideas that are consistent with that growing self-understanding. Not every experiment will take root, and not every idea is congruent with the church's vision of itself; but when it is, and when people with the idea are willing to take leadership and make something happen, leaders need to release control by learning to say "yes." This is what we called in the previous chapter creating a permission-giving culture—and if we are going to find our way into an uncertain future, such a culture needs to flourish.

Finally, leaders can close the loop. It's easy after experiments start and new ways of being in ministry take root, to forget that this process is ongoing and cyclical. Leaders need to keep us asking, "What are we learning from these experiments? How are these actions helping us better understand who we are and what God is doing?" Rather than thinking the planning process has come to an end when the action starts, leaders know that the actions themselves and how the congregation engages in them and what the impacts are can be the beginning places for our next faithful steps in the future, but only if we close the loop; only if we pause, look at what we've done, and ask the right questions. Leaders can see that this happens.

EMBRACING CHAOS

Sometimes the change in our cities feels chaotic; unlike many seemingly unchanging, idyllic rural landscapes, these churches inhabit often noisy, colorful, ever-changing environments. A city is an organism that is constantly evolving. In this context, a church can seek to secure itself *against* this environment by traditional methods of linear and logical strategic planning that guarantee to take us to a new promised land by a sure route. This rarely works.

The other option is to let our own processes mirror our environment, to let the emergence and chaos that makes cities so unique shape our own planning. We can let go of control, and let our planning processes become practices of discernment, through which we listen, learn, discover, and act—trusting that God is giving guidance and perhaps even inviting the upheavals to which we must respond, upheavals that will help us in the end discover new ways of faithfulness in the midst of these cities of God.

DISCUSS THIS:
WHERE ARE YOU ALREADY SEEING EVIDENCE OF GOD'S SPIRIT GUIDING YOUR CONGREGATION? CAN YOU NAME FOUR RISKS YOU MIGHT BE BEING CALLED TO TAKE?

Chapter Four

MISSION AND EVANGELISM: OVERCOMING THE DIVIDE

We are bothered when we see how the church in the United States can't seem to get over the supposed division between what's often called "mission" and "evangelism." We believe evangelism is part of mission, and that the church's mission is to respond to and participate in *all* that God is doing to redeem humanity and heal a broken, wounded world. The split between mission and evangelism infects the church. The split exists within congregations when a congregation has both a mission committee and an evangelism committee that seem to have nothing to do with each other. Worse, there are churches—usually thought of as liberal—that define mission in terms of action for social justice and want to avoid any hint of evangelism, if that means trying to convert people to Christianity; and there are other churches—usually thought of as conservative or evangelical—that focus almost entirely on promoting individual conversions. This is a false dichotomy, something we both learned when we took a class in seminary called "The Local Church in Ministry to God's World."

On the first day of class, South African church leader and retired bishop Peter Storey defined mission as "the active response by a community of believers in obedience to the call of Jesus to share his work in the world."[1] Mission is an act of obedience that always involves a response. We reach out, serve, and love because God reached out, called us by name, served us and loved us. Furthermore, God seeks to accomplish God's work through small groups of people who are willing to faithfully follow God, starting with the Israelites, continuing with the disciples, and ending with the church. The church's main task is to share in Christ's work in the world—and that work includes both inviting people into faith in Christ *and* working for justice, feeding the hungry, and being with the marginalized.

With our attention captured, the class continued with a story called "The Lifeboat Station" by Theodore Wedel.[2] It's a parable of a small lifesaving station on the coast of a sea where numerous shipwrecks occurred. Many devoted members kept watch of the sea, using their one boat to go out and save sailors who became stranded in the dangerous waters. The small station soon became famous for saving lives, and its reputation attracted many people who wanted to be part of their work.

New personalities arrived to the station and concluded that the interior of the building was not up to snuff. They transformed the station with new furniture and a fresh coat of paint, believing they needed a more beautiful space in which to gather and attract more members. Soon, the saving station's crewmembers become more adept at relaxing and enjoying fellowship inside the walls of the beautiful building on the edge of the sea than they were at going out to sea to save people who were drowning. They nearly forgot the entire purpose of their existence.

When a large ship was wrecked off the coast, boatloads of people were brought to the station, but the "property committee" determined that the diverse group of individuals was too dirty to come inside, so showers were constructed outside. As the membership grew, new opinions were formed. Some crewmembers loved the saving station as a place to have fun and meet new people while other crewmembers clung to their mission of saving lives at sea. When the two sides became bitterly divided, a meeting was called to determine whether they would seek out, save, and welcome anyone who needed their help, or provide a clubhouse atmosphere where people could gather for fun. Those members who insisted that the reason they existed was to save lives always found themselves on the losing end of the vote. Still determined to make a difference, they would then go off and start a new saving station only to find that the same division would reoccur after time. While many shipwrecks continue to happen on this coast today, most of the people lost at sea drown—even with a lifeboat station on every block of the shore.

DISCUSS THIS:
HOW DO YOU RELATE TO THIS PARABLE? WHAT DO YOU THINK IT MEANS FOR YOUR CONGREGATION?

We've thought a lot about this parable over the years. Does the faith community you know best focus on providing beautiful space in which people can come in and rest for a while, perhaps an hour or two each week? Or does your faith community focus on making sure drowning people are rescued—both spirituality and physically? What is most striking about this parable is the way it helps the church think about its *one* focus, its *one* mission—to participate in the wide, merciful mission of God.

No churches are better positioned to rediscover the one focus of God's mission—thus reuniting mission and evangelism in a single kingdom vision—than urban churches with their opportunity to creatively address so many human needs, including the need for faith in Christ.

DISCUSS THIS:
HOW WOULD YOU DESCRIBE YOUR CONGREGATION'S PRIMARY FOCUS? IS THERE A DIVIDE BETWEEN MISSION AND EVANGELISM?

MISSION AND EVANGELISM IN SCRIPTURE

There is a strong temptation to grow a church for growth's sake. Some pastors are asked to report each week how many people gathered for worship. Other pastors are asked regularly about the average worship attendance and rarely about the fruit of their ministry or how lives are being touched and transformed. Some pastors have a naturally competitive personality. It's easy to feel the pressure to do everything we can to entice people to come inside our church building, leaving us to believe the secret lies in serving gourmet coffee and having a pastor who wears skinny jeans with a colorful shirt. We stock our shelves with books that tell us how to multiply our membership rolls, at first with good intention but then believing that people exist for the church's needs instead of the church existing for the needs of the people. We follow the advice of church growth experts, and then shake our heads when nothing really happens. But why are we doing what we are doing? And when is the last time we stopped to ask ourselves this question?

Most English Bibles translate the Greek word *euangelos*, from which the word *evangelism* stems, as "gospel." Scott Jones explains, "The prefix *eu* means good and *angelos* means news, so the gospel is the good news of Jesus Christ."[3] Evangelism is sharing the good news of Jesus Christ.

The verb form of the word, *euangelizesthai*, is spoken by Jesus throughout the Gospels. Jesus says, "I must preach the good news of God's kingdom in other cities too, for this is why I was sent" (Luke 4:43). Communicating the good news is an essential part of Jesus's ministry. Jesus is regularly announcing the good news of the kingdom. But Jesus does more than just preach. His proclamation of the good news is often paired with signs and wonders that lead to lives being touched and transformed, and he invites his disciples to do the same.

Jesus calls twelve men and then sends them out on a specific mission. In Matthew's Gospel, immediately after naming the men, Jesus gives them authority to throw out unclean spirits and heal every disease and sickness. "Jesus sent these twelve out and commanded them, 'Don't go among the Gentiles or into a Samaritan city. Go instead to the lost sheep, the people of Israel. As you go, make this announcement: "the kingdom of heaven has come near." Heal the sick, raise the dead, cleanse those with skin diseases, and throw out demons'" (Matt 10:5-8a). A call to offer a specific message is followed by a commandment to do four specific things. Jesus doesn't ask them to get more disciples for the sake of having more disciples. Rather, disciples are to transform lives by healing the sick, raising the dead, cleansing bodies with diseases, and throwing out demons.

In Matthew's Gospel, Jesus travels in cities and villages, "announcing the good news of the kingdom, and healing every disease and every sickness." We then read, "Now when Jesus saw the crowds, he had compassion for them because they were troubled and helpless, like sheep without a shepherd. Then he said to his disciples, 'The size of the harvest is bigger than you can imagine, but there are few workers. Therefore, plead with the Lord of the harvest to send out workers for his harvest'" (Matt 9:35-38). Again, Jesus doesn't request followers. He requests workers who can make a difference in a large harvest where many people are in need of being healed.

Jesus is always moving people into action, reminding people about the work that needs to be done, and giving them the authority required to complete the task. He doesn't ask the disciples to report how many people have come into their midst, gathered for a class, or heard their sermons. He doesn't ask them to share how many new converts have been made. He does, however, make it clear that there are expectations placed upon them. Following Jesus entails making a tangible difference in the world.

In the book of Acts, the Holy Spirit comes, just as Jesus promised the disciples it would. The gathered individuals are filled with the Spirit and begin to speak in other languages, leading some pious Jews to believe the crowd is filled with new wine. With accusations flying, Peter stands and explains how Joel's prophecy is fulfilled before sharing how Jesus, who was killed on a cross, has been raised to life. He declares Jesus as Lord and Christ, leaving those in the crowd questioning what they should do in response. An invitation is given for them to change their hearts and lives, and three thousand people are brought into the community on that day through baptism (Acts 2:41).

Peter's preaching of the good news is the mechanism through which thousands of individuals come to know Jesus. His words cut through their confused hearts, leading them to want to change their lives. Those who hear his message don't return home and continue to live as they did before their baptism, however. Quite the contrary: "The believers devoted themselves to the apostles' teaching, to the community, to their shared meals, and to their prayers" (Acts 2:42). This behavior leads to a sense of awe coming upon everyone as many signs and wonders are being done. The believers pooled their possessions, seeking to meet whatever needs existed in the community. They worshipped together in the temple and gladly shared their food. "They praised God and demonstrated God's goodness to everyone. The Lord added daily to the community those who were being saved" (Acts 2:47). People were added to the community because of the community's embodiment of the good news.

MISSION AND EVANGELISM TOGETHER

If mission and evangelism aren't radically distinct in scripture, then it should be no surprise that many missiologists try to bring the two back together. David J. Bosch defines evangelism as "that dimension and activity of the church's mission which seeks to offer every person, everywhere, a valid opportunity to be directly challenged by the gospel of explicit faith in Jesus Christ, with a view to embracing him as Savior, becoming a living member of his community, and being enlisted in his service of reconciliation, peace, and justice on earth."[4] Communities of people who are faithfully seeking reconciliation, peace, and justice can't help but confront the individuals around them as they embody a different way of living and loving. The visible embodiment of love, faith, hope, and justice is irresistible to many individuals, leaving them wanting to be a part of the new thing God is doing.

TRY THIS:
ON A LARGE SHEET OF PAPER, LIST ALL THE MINISTRIES OF YOUR CONGREGATION YOU CONSIDER TO BE "MISSION" AND ALL THE ONES YOU CONSIDER TO BE "EVANGELISM." WHAT DO YOU LEARN ABOUT YOUR CONGREGATION FROM THE LISTS? HOW ARE THE TWO LISTS RELATED?

People became a part of the early church because individuals carefully followed Jesus's instructions to make a difference. Formerly diseased and demon-possessed individuals responded by following Jesus. People who saw a community living differently wanted to become a part of it, and several people repented, making a decision to live a changed life in the process. Mission and evangelism were intrinsically connected. One could not happen without the other.

DISCUSS THIS:
WHAT STRUCTURES IN YOUR CONGREGATION SUPPORT MISSION AND EVANGELISM? HOW ARE THEY RELATED?

Why, then, do we too often separate mission and evangelism into two distinct functions of the church with a ministry team or committee for each one? What might happen if we were to combine the two again, making sure our proclamation of the good news is always accompanied by efforts to heal bodies, minds, and spirits, and fix unjust social systems, instead of growing a church for growth's sake? The following two churches are figuring out how.

All Peoples Church was founded in 1991 as a multicultural congregation in the Harambee community of Milwaukee, Wisconsin. A 2014 article in the *Milwaukee Journal Sentinel* described the congregation: "Half of the 220 or so members are younger than 25. And many are active in liturgy, in the garden and orchard that are the foundations of its food justice ministry, even in church governance." The articles notes that in 2011, All Peoples elected its youngest president: an eighteen-year-old aspiring hip-hop artist.[5] All Peoples is a thriving, growing congregation that is making an impact in its community. But that wasn't always the case.

Reverend Steve Jerbi, the church's senior pastor, describes how the building they occupy was first constructed to house Epiphany Lutheran Church in 1906. The congregation grew and flourished before diminishing when its neighborhood started to change. With thirty or so members remaining, the church closed in 1990. One year later, All Peoples was started, placing an immediate emphasis on the youth and young adults in the Harambee community located two miles from downtown Milwaukee.

Harambee is a Swahili word that means, "Let's pull together." Like many predominantly African-American communities in the United States, Harambee is experiencing rapid redevelopment and gentrification, making the church's role to pull people together even more critical. The congregation was committed from the very beginning to reducing food insecurity and now has a greenhouse and an orchard to help produce fresh fruits and vegetables that can be distributed throughout the community. Freedom School, a six-week day camp rooted in the Civil Rights movement, is offered each summer. Neighbors know about All Peoples because of the difference it makes in their lives, and they respond by becoming involved in the life of the congregation. In fact, Reverend Jerbi reports that 75 percent of the church's membership came to the church first through its programs for the community. The congregation tripled in size during Reverend Jerbi's leadership, and the predominantly younger than twenty-five crowd makes All Peoples Church an exception in the Evangelical Lutheran Church of America. A congregation committed to serving young people can quickly become filled with young people who are also looking for places to serve and make a difference. Missional service and evangelism clearly go hand in hand.

TRY THIS:
INTERVIEW FIVE YOUNG PEOPLE UNDER TWENTY-FIVE IN YOUR CONGREGATION AND ASK THEM WHAT DIFFERENCE THE CHURCH MAKES IN THEIR LIVES. DO THE SAME THING WITH THE FIVE NEWEST MEMBERS. THEN DISCUSS WHAT THIS TEACHES YOU ABOUT YOUR CONGREGATION.

When asked about mission and evangelism, William H. Lamar IV, senior pastor of Metropolitan African Methodist Episcopal Church, in Washington, DC, states with a laugh, "Jesus wouldn't recognize 'door knocking' as gospel!" The laughter accompanying this statement is then replaced with great intentionality as he adds, "Jesus invites us to be a part of the new creation."

Bishop Richard Allen founded the African Methodist Episcopal Church in 1787 to provide the community of Africans in Philadelphia with a place to worship on their own terms. Bishop

Allen formed the church and started to work toward a new creation while providing a place of hope and joy for African Americans.

Metropolitan has been working toward this new creation since its founding in 1838. Mission and evangelism have always been one in the same at Metropolitan AME as the church's focus has remained worship, liberation, and service. Lamar explains, "If there is justice, there is no need for services for the victims of injustice." But with injustice everywhere, the congregation has always had plenty to do as it seeks to fight oppression. Today, the church fights dislocation of African Americans in the city, what Lamar calls "a new form of colonialism." His congregation is also committed to working for better education, housing, and living wages in Washington, DC. Lamar can't immediately tell you what the average worship attendance is for his congregation. Rather, he evaluates success as a congregation on whether they are making a difference in education, housing, wages, and other efforts targeting injustices. He points out how "God is committed to the flourishing of this place only when we are committed to the flourishing of human beings."[6]

DISCUSS THIS:
IN WHAT WAYS IS YOUR CONGREGATION SIMILAR OR DISSIMILAR TO THE TWO CONGREGATIONS DISCUSSED IN THIS SECTION? WHAT CAN YOU LEARN FROM THEM?

Imagine what might happen—what God might do with and through you and your congregation—if your primary focus became the flourishing of humanity in all its many dimensions: spiritual, physical, social.

HOW DO WE PRACTICE BOTH TODAY?

It's not popular to be a Christian today.

The number of "nones," those who claim no religious affiliation, has increased to an all-time high, making it the second largest "religious" group in our country, and the "none" population continues to grow at an alarming rate. One in three college-aged adults has given up on organized religion altogether, and the church is projected to lose more than half its members who are in their twenties who once believed the church and Christianity were important components of their life.[7]

This backdrop makes us savor the research from a 2015 Pew survey on urban Christianity. According to this data, out of the largest metro areas in our nation, only San Francisco has a population that is less than 50 percent Christian.[8] One thing is clear: the church still has both plenty of people to work with and plenty of people to reach!

But where do we begin?

When the archives at Mount Vernon Place were being reorganized, a church member came across an article clipped from the September 18, 1950, issue of *The Washington Post*. The article was written the day after a beloved pastor, John Rustin, preached his final sermon as pastor. Rustin served the congregation from 1936–1950, using his visionary leadership to grow the congregation to more than four thousand members. He was known for his ability to always remember a name and for creating space for young adults to gather and grow in their faith. But the article points to an even greater reason for why the church may have attracted hundreds of new people during his tenure.

The article describes how Rustin told the "misty-eyed gathering of more than 1,500 persons" how the church is not liberal enough. The article, written by Thomas Schlesinger, a *Washington Post* reporter, reads:

> Doctor Rustin told the congregation, "the trouble with the church is that it is not liberal enough," and then spelled out what he thought the church of the future should be like. "When the church becomes a real factor in the life of the people," he said, "first of all, it has vision and is not expending all its energy in defending creeds or standing on ancient dogmas. It should challenge the people to move beyond its warped emotions and deep-seated prejudices," he continued, "and it should always move into action."[9]

Though labels like "liberal" are increasingly irrelevant, it is an important question to ask: What does a church that has become a real factor in people's lives look like?

Washington, DC's Church of the Saviour provides countless examples. Jim Wallace writes about how the church's founder, Gordon Cosby, spent his life thinking about "What actually is this thing called church supposed to look like, act like, and be like in the lives of ordinary people and ordinary communities?"[10]

Cosby's leadership and commitment to the poor created a remarkable church—not a mega-church with big, high-tech facilities—but a unique church that gathers in rather humble locations around the metropolitan area of Washington. Michelle Boorstein of *The Washington Post* writes, "The Church of the Saviour was never a conventional church. It has no pews, no Sunday school, not even a Christmas service. Instead, for 60 years this small, unusual group based in Northwest Washington has quietly fueled a revolution in faith-based activism." Boorstein notes the impact of

Church of the Saviour on the community: "One of its programs found jobs for 800 people [in 2008]. Another provided 325 units of affordable housing. There's Columbia Road Health Services. Christ House medical services for the homeless. Miriam's House for women with AIDS. And on and on."[11]

In 1956, some nine years after the Church of the Saviour was born, Cosby reflected with these words:

> I believe the only hope of our world is the existence of Christian communities which are completely real, in which there is no artificiality, no equivocation. We must come to the place where we can do what Jesus did, where we can watch the rich young ruler walk away and, with sorrow and ache in our hearts, let him go until he can come back on the terms of Jesus Christ. We have been so afraid we might lose potential members that we have been willing to take them on their own terms. Then we wonder why the church is relatively impotent and doesn't have the power to transform human life, to shake society at its very roots.[12]

Articulating a vision as we described it in chapter 2, Cosby understood that becoming a real factor in people's lives required setting high standards for what it means to follow Jesus: redefining wealth, showing up, eating together, and meeting tangible needs. While Cosby died in 2013, the church he founded continues to play a vital role in the lives of countless people living in Washington.

In his book *Being Church*, John Alexander claims that a church wins people to what the church wins them with.[13] Cosby won people to compassion, humility, and sacrificial service through ministries that met people where they were and journeyed with them to wholeness.

Any congregation in decline may be tempted to believe they can win people with high-energy worship, creative PowerPoint presentations, and better music. You may very well be able to boost your average worship attendance with such methods. But there is a far more powerful way of winning people and it starts with embodying the new commandment Jesus gives to his disciples in the Gospel of John: "Love each other. Just as I have loved you, so you also must love each other. This is how everyone will know that you are my disciples, when you love each other" (John 13:34-35).

When love is faithfully embodied, it not only transforms people and communities but also attracts people to be part of our communities. Fortunately, the love of Christ can also be embodied in a myriad of ways and in every context no matter who is in your congregation and what city you find yourself in.

BEING WITH

Samuel Wells writes,

> There is no value in being unless it is being with. There is no value in existence unless it is existence in relationship—with God, one another, and the creation. The heaven that is worth aspiring to is a rejoining of such relationship, a restoration of community, a discovery of partnership, a sense of being in the presence of another in which there is neither a folding of identities that loses their difference nor a sharpening of difference that leads to hostility, but an enjoyment of the other that evokes cherishing and relishing. The theological word for this is communion.[14]

Communion—real communion with each other and the wider community—can transform a church.

When I (Donna) was preparing to come to Mount Vernon Place, one person told me I would be a "hospice chaplain" to the older members while "starting a new church" with the young adults moving into the neighborhood. I soon learned that the words, while meant in a helpful way, couldn't be further from the truth.

Not long after the congregation finally started to attract new young adults, I received a call from a young woman who had been coming to worship with her husband for a few months. Kris and Kristine were in the process of purchasing a condominium when their closing date was delayed. They had already given their thirty-day notice to their current landlord and needed a place to stay for a couple of weeks. I suggested that they call Ruth, a ninety-year-old widow who lived close to public transportation and had an extra room in her home. They called Ruth, explained their situation, and Ruth welcomed them into her home. The two weeks turned into four weeks. Four weeks turned into a total of three months. In that time, Kris and Kristine met all of Ruth's friends, including many of the longtime members of the church, while Ruth met many of the new people who had started coming to her beloved church. It was an unlikely community of people living together, but the experience was enough to help Kris and Kristine discern that they were being called to purchase a four-bedroom home where they could continue to live in intentional community.

Today, several church members have lived with Kris, Kristine, and their young son. Different people experiencing homelessness have also been welcomed to stay for a while. When one family in our congregation was facing foreclosure, Kris and Kristine gave generously to prevent the foreclosure from happening, sharing that "when we were faced with the potential of not having a place to live, someone in this church welcomed us and provided us with a place to call home." Kris is the main facilitator of a Tuesday morning group that provides housing and employment resources. The light shining from this couple through their ability to love like Jesus has helped shape the culture of the entire congregation while also expanding the congregation's ministry with the city and especially people who are facing homelessness. It all started with a ninety-year-old who was willing to open her home. Her *being with* this young couple made a profound impact on the congregation's capacity to be with the community and one another.

The church isn't called to knock on doors or extend invitations for the sake of packing the pews. The church is called to give life, to make a difference in the lives of individuals and the world. We are disciples of Jesus Christ not because of a decision we have made but because of the lives we live, the ministry we embody. We make disciples of Jesus Christ not by extending an invitation to come and join us but by being like Jesus—a tangible, visible, audible body offering a glimpse of God's reign around us.

Chapter Five

GIVING OUR BEST: NOT AFRAID OF EXCELLENCE

Y ou might not immediately turn to a steakhouse to learn how small details make an enormous difference, but two restaurants that "sweat the small stuff" may inspire you to think differently.

The Angus Barn in Raleigh, North Carolina, has garnered dozens of accolades since opening in 1960. The family-owned business is regularly packed with patrons who are willing to splurge on a memorable meal that is perfect for one of life's celebrations. A quick glance at the restaurant's website reveals the owner's commitment to hospitality: "Be it a wedding proposal, that special 80th birthday, a business meeting or simply a family night out, this time that we have is our chance to make [the customer] feel like the most important person in the world."[1] Van Eure, current owner and daughter of founder Thad Eure, understands how customers have the capacity to keep the doors of her business open by returning to eat at the Angus Barn or close them by taking their business to another dining establishment. The attention to detail is tangible the moment you step on the property and continues until you've walked out the door.

A family member started a conversation with Van during a visit to the restaurant years ago. Van shared information about the source of their beef and practices for hiring. She described how she sometimes sets an empty soft drink can on the front steps of the restaurant prior to a prospective employee's interview. If the prospective employee stops and picks up the can, Van knows the person is worth considering for a role in the restaurant. If the person picks up the can, then he or she will regularly seek to notice the small details that can make or break a diner's experience. If a prospective employee walks by the can, Van cuts the interview short.

Are the pastors, staff, and leaders in your congregation in the practice of paying attention to details? Do you understand how one small thing can be the tipping point that can either bring someone back into your doors or prevent a first-time guest from returning to your church?

Halls Chophouse is a premier, award-winning steakhouse in Charleston, South Carolina. Opened in 2009, the Hall Family has not had as many years to perfect their practice as the Angus Barn. But perfection is what you experience the moment you step inside. Guests are greeted by name by the hostess. A member of the Hall family may be there to take your coat while another employee guides you to your table, letting you know how glad she is that you're there. The food is served with pride. When the meal is over, guests are invited to share comments and contact information on a card that arrives with the check. If you complete the card and offer your contact information, you will find a note in your mailbox thanking you for coming to the restaurant, a note that sometimes arrives before you've even made it home from Charleston.

How does your congregation follow up with people who visit the church? If you are the pastor, do you write a note or make a call within hours of a person showing up to worship for the first time? Do you require yourself, members of your team, or people in your congregation to follow up with anyone who left their contact information? Or do people who visit your church leave their contact information only to never hear another word?

Of course, the church isn't a restaurant, but that doesn't mean we can't learn from any organization that pays attention to excellence, treats people well, and knows that little things matter. Urban congregations seeking renewal have an obvious place to begin: striving for excellence in all they do.

BEING THE BEST—OR NOT

When Stanley Hauerwas was named "America's Best Theologian" by *Time* in 2011, he responded by saying that best is not a theological category.[2] Best is not of God because to be the best means one has triumphed or been exalted over others. We conclude that the "best" team won while knowing that another team is just as good but didn't play as well on a particular day. There is one "best" man at a wedding, but the groom could feel equally close to the three other friends standing by his side. We don't worship a God who lifts some people up as the "best" but rather a God who adores all of creation. Similarly, we aren't called to be the "best" church in our community, but we are called to embody excellence and greatness in all we do as congregations.

What does it look like for the church to offer its best or embody greatness? When Paul writes to the Philippians from prison, he shares, "It is my expectation and hope that I won't be put to shame in anything. Rather, I hope with daring courage that Christ's greatness will be seen in my body, now as always, whether I live or die" (Phil 1:20). He then called the Philippians to "live together in a manner worthy of Christ's gospel" (1:28).

How would you respond to the question, "What makes Jesus great?"

You might think about his extraordinary capacity to see individuals, meeting them right where they are. You might ponder his sacrificial love that was demonstrated through giving his all, even life itself. You might gravitate toward his humility, his capacity to empty himself and become like one of us. You might imagine his desire always to watch out for others, doing what he can to provide what they need. You may think about how he was tempted in every way but was without sin. Whatever comes to mind, Jesus offered his full self, his very best self.

Jesus is not only the object of our affection as Christians, he is our model for how to live. We are called to live a life worthy of the good news Jesus preached and embodied. According to Paul, such a life entails embodying faithfulness and courage, having the same love of Christ, and thinking of others as better than we think of ourselves. Paul later writes, "From now on, brothers and sisters, if anything is excellent and if anything is admirable, focus your thoughts on these things: all that is true, all that is holy, all that is just, all that is pure, all that is lovely, and all that is worthy of praise" (Phil 4:8).

DISCUSS THIS:
WHERE IN YOUR CONGREGATION'S LIFE DOES EXCELLENCE MATTER? WHERE DOES MEDIOCRITY PREVAIL?

How are you seeking to live lives worthy of the gospel as an individual and as a congregation? How is your life a reflection of the good news proclaimed and embodied by Jesus? Are you striving for excellence or settling for mediocrity?

WHAT DIFFERENCE DOES EXCELLENCE MAKE?

Pastor Nadia Bolz-Weber once said of her congregation, "We're anti-excellence, and pro-participation."[3] As much as we admire her work and the work of her congregation, on this point we disagree: excellence is essential.

When asked how much excellence matters, Amy Butler, senior pastor at New York City's Riverside Church, immediately responded, "It matters 150 percent to me. This is the family of God. We are the community of Christ. Why would we give God anything less?"[4]

Since coming to Riverside in 2014, Butler sought to give her best while recruiting staff and leaders who would do the same. She knows that change happens from the inside out, and she built a team of staff and lay leaders who exhibit health and model faithfulness to the congregation and the world. She equates the role of a pastor and church leader to being a parent, noting how members of the congregation watch those in paid leadership positions all the time, and she wants people to see lives that are worthy of the gospel.

Butler has three rules for every staff member and member of the Riverside Church Council: do excellent work, keep communication lines open all the time, and make sure there are no surprises. To encourage excellence and an entrepreneurial spirit, Butler created an "excellence fund." Staff members can apply for grants of up to one thousand dollars each to fund travel or experiences that will help them be more effective in their roles. One staff member received a grant to spend four days in Key West, Florida, to write a plan for communications and design a new logo. Butler knows that a staff that is nurtured, cared for, and encouraged to try new things is a staff that will continue to live into the high standards she sets.

In addition to seeking excellence from her staff, Butler points out countless places where the congregation could do better. When Butler arrived at Riverside, instead of what she describes as "cathedral warmth," she felt an oppressive air to the massive building that was partially planned and funded by John D. Rockefeller. She set out to do whatever it took to make sure every public space in the building projected the ideal of loving community. The current lightbulbs were exchanged for bulbs with a higher wattage to make the space brighter. Full-color pictures of the congregation were placed around the facility, showcasing the Riverside Church congregation for any visitor who steps inside the building. Air fresheners made every space smell good. Candy jars were strategically placed in offices and filled with chocolates that beckoned people to come in, creating community and building relationships. Butler knows small details make an enormous difference.

EMBODYING EXCELLENCE

Excellence can be sought and embodied in every ministry at the church. From maintaining facilities to welcoming guests, planning and leading worship to expressing gratitude, aiming for excellence is a way of saying that these little things matter, because the people who worship here matter and those who are yet to come matter. If God is so concerned with details that God counts the number of hairs on one's head, then the least we can do is aim for excellence. Below we discuss seven areas of a congregation's life and ministry where excellence can be pursued. Striving for excellence never stops, but these are places to begin.

LEADERSHIP

In his 2001 *New York Times* bestseller *Good to Great*, Jim Collins illustrates why some companies make it and others do not. Collins skips over the mediocrity stage and criticizes any company that settles for being good when greatness is achievable. Collins would affirm the importance of pruning (as we suggested in chapter 1) and how what we stop doing is just as important as what we continue to do. He then offers additional lessons for the church to ponder and put to practice, particularly around staffing and leadership.

People are pivotal to the success of any organization, and getting the right people in the right positions is essential. Collins uses the image of a bus, suggesting that we first get the right people on the bus and then discern what seat they should occupy.[5] Our congregations also need the right leadership on the bus, people who are given a role not because of how long they have been a member of the church or their winsome personality, but because of the servanthood they embody, the gifts they bring, and the ways they seek to live a life worthy of the gospel. Leaders should be people who are not only showing up but people who are embodying faithful discipleship when it comes to the giving of time, talent, and financial resources, as well as practicing spiritual disciplines. Individuals cannot lead people to do what they are not yet doing.

Excellence in leadership means considering seriously the following questions: To what are your church's leaders accountable? Are there certain standards that must be met before someone is given a leadership role? What might happen if leaders were required to be in worship three out of four Sundays of the month, to give sacrificially while working toward a tithe (if they are not already giving 10 percent of their income), to pray for the church daily, and to be in a small group or Bible study where they are growing in their faith? Who might be qualified if the church only selected individuals who are practicing their faith in tangible ways?

DISCUSS THIS:
HOW DO YOU FEEL ABOUT THE IDEA OF LEADERS BEING ACCOUNTABLE TO CERTAIN STANDARDS OF PARTICIPATION?

TRY THIS:
BRAINSTORM AS A GROUP WHAT MIGHT BE APPROPRIATE STANDARDS OF EXCELLENCE FOR LEADERS IN YOUR CONGREGATION.

Leadership teams should consist of people who are committed to going the extra mile; to showing up even when it's hard to show up; to seeing what is not yet visible; to picking up the soda can on the front lawn; to going out of their way to welcome a newcomer; to serving even if they're not assigned a role for that day; and perhaps most importantly, to discerning God's direction as they seek to lead. Once it's clear who has a heart for God, people, and the church, then they can fill the right role in which their gifts can be used to make a difference in your community.

THE FACILITY

Striving for excellence starts outside the doors, before someone walks inside the church building. Downtown Washington, DC, used to be filled with surface parking lots that were overflowing with people who drove downtown for work before returning home to the suburbs. The surface parking lots started to disappear not long after the turn of this century. It soon became impossible to walk or drive downtown without seeing a dozen construction cranes playing a role in the creation of luxury apartment buildings, trophy office buildings, or condominiums that would soon have the distinction of selling for more per square foot than any other neighborhood in the city. Meanwhile, church buildings that were erected at the turn of the last century were showing their age on nearly every city block. A clergy coach asked, "How do you expect people who are paying a premium to live in your neighborhood to want to come inside your church if you have not done anything to make your outside more attractive?" This question motivated the trustees at one church to make a larger investment in landscaping, making sure that not only the lawn is well kept but that colorful flowers are changed throughout each season as well.

It's not just people paying a premium who live near urban congregations. People of all income levels pass by our church buildings each day—on the bus, on foot, or while stopping on the steps to rest. And folks without homes often find rest and take shelter near our church buildings. They, too, deserve to be greeted by a beautiful, well-maintained facility. The wealthy might expect flowers; those who are experiencing poverty might be honored by them.

So consider these questions as you think about excellence and the facility:

- What do people see when they approach your building?

- Is the outside well maintained?

- Are there signs that help people find their way inside?

- Is the marquee up to date?

- And what happens when someone steps inside your church building?

- Is the bathroom always clean and ready for use?

- Is furniture neat and tidy, inviting people to sit and stay for a while?

- What does your church smell like?

DISCUSS THIS:
WHAT ARE THREE SIMPLE THINGS YOU COULD DO TO IMPROVE THE HOSPITALITY AND APPEARANCE OF YOUR CHURCH BUILDING?

Numerous church buildings are so full of stuff that it looks like the congregation recently had a yard sale and brought all the unsold merchandise inside. Whether it's extra chairs or china the church is always receiving goods from people who often assume the church wants whatever they no longer need. The congregation then regularly believes it can move into a different future without letting go of anything. But no one moves into a new house without taking several trips to the local Goodwill. What would it take to provide a fresh look to your space: flowers, a coat of paint, new carpet, less junk, more attractive furniture, a candy jar overflowing with chocolate?

TRY THIS:
GET A GROUP TOGETHER AND DO THE THREE THINGS
YOU DISCUSSED ABOVE.

HOSPITALITY

A colleague was on maternity leave when she tried to visit a church one Sunday. When she arrived at the entrance of the parking garage, she noticed a large sign that said, "Parking Reserved for Office Tenants Only." She drove past and went around the block a few times looking for a parking space before returning home, frustrated that she had driven downtown but was unable to park. She quickly shared her experience with the pastor in an e-mail, writing, "I tried to come to your church, but the parking garage was already full." The parking garage wasn't full, however. Rather, the signs placed at the entrance of the garage were put out every Sunday as a way for the garage owner to inform other drivers that the parking garage was not open for ordinary business. The regular worshippers knew that the garage is always open to people coming to church on Sundays no matter what the signs say. But how would a first-time guest know they were welcome to park in the garage if the sign said otherwise? Who knows how many people tried to visit the church only to be turned away! Can first-time guests easily find their way into your church building? Do people know where to park and what entrance to use or do you assume people can find their way?

What does a guest experience once inside? Nearly every congregation claims to be friendly, even priding themselves on their friendliness. But are guests warmly welcomed, handed a bulletin, shown to a seat, and then accompanied to coffee hour? Or do guests come inside, sit quietly, and wait for someone to notice them only to leave without speaking to anyone? Are greeters always looking for a newcomer or regularly talking amongst themselves? One of the most important prayers we can pray whenever we gather for worship is, "Dear God, please help everyone who comes to be noticed in a real and tangible way," and then seek to embody the answer to this prayer in as many ways as possible.

How do you follow up with guests? Like Halls Chophouse, if you are a pastor do you write a note to every guest who leaves their contact information, expressing your gratitude before you leave the office on Sundays? Or do people who leave their contact information never hear from anyone? Do you have a notepad that is passed down each pew, one that regular worshippers only sign their name in because you know them, so guests follow their lead, leaving you unable to connect with them? When a guest returns for a second or third visit, do you invite them to share coffee or lunch with you in an effort to get to know their story while connecting them with your church's ministries?

Here's a simple practice that can transform a church's ability to connect with people: replace pads that everyone signs with three different colored connect cards: one for guests, one for friends, and one for members. Guest cards give people the opportunity to indicate whether it is their first, second, or third time worshipping with you, making it easy to identify your first-time visitors. Guest cards also ask how someone found out about your church, enabling you to see if any advertising efforts are making a difference and gauge the effectiveness of your website and social media campaigns. Member cards have a place for people to update their contact information while guest and friend cards ask for contact information. All cards have a place for people to offer prayer requests as well as space to write a message to the pastor. Every person is invited to complete a card as part of the opening announcements and then put it in the offering plate later in the service of worship while being reminded that our presence is a gift we offer to the people sitting in the pews with us as well as to God.

DISCUSS THIS:
HOW DOES YOUR CHURCH SYSTEMATICALLY FOLLOW UP WITH GUESTS? HOW COULD YOU IMPROVE YOUR CURRENT PRACTICES?

In some areas, people might be delighted to have you show up on their doorstep with a coffee mug and a word of gratitude for coming. In many urban areas, it can be hard to get past the condo or apartment building security person to greet guests. However, the pastor sending a thank-you e-mail to guests can be equally effective. And don't underestimate how many guests might take you up on your invitation to have coffee or lunch later in the week. People who live in concrete condominium buildings where they don't know the name of their next-door neighbor whose bedroom is separated by only a wall are often yearning to be noticed and experience real, authentic connection.

FINANCIAL GENEROSITY AND STEWARDSHIP

If you make a $100 donation to your undergraduate college or university, the local humane society, or a nearby shelter for women, there is a good chance you will receive a thank-you note from the development office or a staff member of the organization before the month has ended. But many of us have been going to church for years, sometimes giving the church thousands of dollars each year, and we have never received a thank-you note—not even with the computer-generated statement of giving that arrives in time for our income taxes to be filed. In fact, the church may be the only non-profit organization in the community that relies upon its constituents' generosity where a person can write a check for $10,000 and never receive a personal note of gratitude.

Every person who makes a financial pledge to your church should receive a handwritten thank-you note at a minimum. Some churches give every person who makes a pledge a gift such as a coffee mug, water bottle, or umbrella bearing the church's name. At one church, a family made a pledge because they wanted to receive mugs like everyone else.

The practice of mailing mid-year financial updates to people who have pledged with a letter describing some of the ways God is perceived to be working within and through the congregation can also be a powerful way of expressing gratitude while also encouraging people to continue to give or catch up on their commitment. While end-of-year giving statements can be easily e-mailed, a more effective practice is to add to each statement a letter that outlines specific fruit that has been cultivated over the last twelve months through the generosity of the congregation, with a personal note added by the pastor.

One additional practice to express gratitude to givers while encouraging generosity is to gather the top tier givers for a meal during which the pastor can offer personal thanksgiving. After all, we go out of our way to encourage and appreciate people with all kinds of gifts; it's appropriate to show appreciation for those who have the gift of generosity as well.

It is also important for people to know how the church is using its resources. Communicating a congregation's financial priorities shouldn't happen once a year when the pastor is on her knees begging God to help people pledge more money to meet the budget for the coming year. A helpful way of communicating is through personal testimony time. An individual whose life has been affected by a specific ministry at the church can be invited to stand and articulate with passion how he came to the church, where he's been affected by the congregation, and how his life has been transformed through its people or ministries. A pastor or layperson in worship leadership can then respond to the testimony by sharing words that remind the congregation how giving is a spiritual discipline, inviting the congregation to give regularly, intentionally, and generously before making the connection of how a portion of what they give will go to strengthening the ministry they have just heard about—a ministry that is clearly touching and transforming lives. Jesus talks about money more than any other matter. Why do we believe we should only talk about money during stewardship season, or even worse, one Sunday a year?

Information on the budget and how to embody financial generosity should be included in every new member class. You may decide to include a line item budget of where each dollar goes. Another effective way of communicating the budget if you are a part of a congregation that is particularly generous or deeply involved in mission work is to present the budget in the form of a pie chart that includes the percentage you spend on missions, education, children, staff, worship, facility costs, and anything else. Many people haven't been part of congregations that are transparent in their spending and use of financial resources, making transparency a welcome gift that leads individuals to trust the church with a larger percentage of their resources.

CHILDREN'S MINISTRY

Troy and his family started their search for a new church home immediately after moving to a new city. They arrived at one church early with their young child, wanting to make sure they had plenty of time to locate the children's ministry area, get their son settled, and then find the sanctuary. The person at the front doors showed them how to get to the appropriate classroom for his age, and they made their way downstairs. When they found the room, there was a father and his two sons inside. No appointed childcare workers were there, even though it was twenty minutes before the start of worship. The father of the two boys welcomed them and said, "You can leave your son with me. Our childcare workers are late today." Troy and his wife reluctantly accepted his invitation.

While Troy and his family never returned to the church, they did take time to write the pastor. "My wife and I didn't hear a word you preached on Sunday because all we could think about is how we had left our child with a complete stranger. We were eager to visit, but no one was ready to receive us when we arrived." Their opinion of the church was formed within five minutes of walking inside the door. The church wasn't ready to receive this new family because the children's ministry staff was tardy. Two people arriving ten minutes late prevented people from being able to see and experience God in worship while helping to encourage the couple to keep looking for a church that would be prepared to welcome their child. Our congregations are rarely offered a second chance to make a good first impression.

Troy is now leading the children's ministry at an urban congregation located six blocks from the United States Capitol. In this role, he seeks to embody the excellence he longs to find whenever he visits other churches. Many of his teachers are personally invited to serve by Troy because of their participation in an adult Bible study where Troy has watched them grow in their own faith. Volunteers are individually trained by Troy, learning the importance of process, pedagogy, cleanliness, calling a child by name, and making sure parents feel their child is safe and secure. Troy sends birthday cards to each child on their birthday and a letter to children on the anniversary of their baptism that reminds them how God and the congregation dearly loves them. The church's ministry with children doubled under his leadership in just three years. Troy knows excellence and details matter!

How does your paid and unpaid ministry staff greet children? Are they always on time? Are your children's classrooms always clean? Do you affirm children on their birthday and baptism anniversary day? How do people know who the paid and volunteer workers are? Are they easily identifiable?

The transformational children's curriculum known as Godly Play has a "threshold moment" that children cross each time they come to Sunday school. A volunteer is at the door, ready to greet them, call them by name, and share how excited she is to have them there. While we may not all offer Godly Play, all of us can be prepared to welcome children as our honored guests.

TRY THIS:
LIST FIVE OTHER AREAS OF A CHURCH'S LIFE WHERE EXCELLENCE CAN BE PURSUED, THEN DISCUSS WHAT EXCELLENCE MIGHT LOOK LIKE IN EACH OF THEM.

STRIVING FOR GREATNESS

Jim Collins tells the story of Dave Scott, a world-class athlete who won countless triathlons. Dave could bike, swim, and run long distances at a pace that would make many of our heads spin. Dave was fit and in shape. He didn't need to lose any weight. But Dave still paid attention to details as small as rinsing his cottage cheese in order to remove the extra fat.[6] How much fat could cling to a few kernels of cottage cheese? It is hard to imagine that the fat on cottage cheese amounts to much. But everything, even something as insignificant as a tiny bit of extra fat, made a difference to Dave.

What if the details of what we do, even those that seem so insignificant, also play a role in what we are able to achieve, who we are able to serve, and who we are able to reach?

Will you pay attention to the small stuff?

DISCUSS THIS:
WHAT ARE FIVE CHANGES YOU'RE WILLING TO MAKE IMMEDIATELY TO EMBODY EXCELLENCE? WHAT, IF ANYTHING, IS PREVENTING YOU FROM MAKING THESE CHANGES?

Chapter Six

PRESENT YOUR BODIES: THE WORSHIP CONVERSATION

A TALE OF THREE CHURCHES

C *hurch Number One:* I (Roger) am the guest preacher at a tall steeple church. The long sanctuary with a center aisle is painted white. Clear windows let in some morning light. White columns range along the side aisle. A hundred or so people sparsely populate the hard wooden pews in a space designed to hold four times that many. The opening words of worship are read by one of the clergy who also speaks the opening prayer. The congregation sings two hymns and says in unison the prayer of confession. There is a brief time of greeting neighbors. A medium-sized choir with paid soloists sings exquisite sacred music.

Because I planned to preach on the baptism of Jesus, I suggested this might be a good day to have a congregation-wide reaffirmation of baptismal vows, one of my favorite liturgical acts when I was a pastor. I loved standing behind the baptismal font and watching parishioners stream out of their pews and down the aisles to touch the water. Some marked the sign of the cross on their foreheads, others splashed their faces as if rinsing after a shave. Still others simply dipped the tips of their fingers in the water.

So I expect something similar here. One of the clergy stands behind the baptismal font, prays a prayer of blessing, touches the water, and declares, "Remember your baptism and be thankful!" then sits down. The rest of us watch from our seats. We never speak, move, or touch the water.

Some might look at this service and say, "That's the problem with traditional worship! No wonder the sanctuary isn't full." But we don't think the problem is the style of worship.

Church Number Two: A thriving downtown congregation in a large city. A thousand people worship each Sunday at three different services. When other churches in its situation are declining, this Presbyterian congregation has bucked the trend, experiencing growth in every measurable way. Duke Memorial was considering starting a second service, so a planning group attends this congregation's contemporary "praise and worship" service. In the enormous renovated fellowship hall, the finest musicians stand on a stage and play the latest contemporary music. We sing along for fifteen minutes at the beginning. The sermon, casual and conversational, is supported by well-timed images and videos projected on a screen.

I brought the team to this service because I knew it would be done with excellence. Their assessment? They were bored. Even though this service had contributed to the church's growth, a member of my team summed up her reaction: "After we sang, we just sat there." Some would say, "That's the problem with contemporary worship—it's just show."

Church Number Three: A relatively young congregation renting a space on the border between a residential neighborhood and downtown Durham, North Carolina. They meet for worship on Sunday evenings. When you enter, you see a few icons, then notice chairs set up in the round in the high-ceilinged worship space. Eventually about a hundred people fill the chairs as worship begins. The worship leaders, situated in the middle of the circle of chairs, confesses that the opening song will be difficult to sing—he wrote it, and the singer-songwriter style of the melody is tricky to follow. But the congregation seems intent on catching the tune and articulating the lyrics. After the beginning song, the congregation passes the peace, and the pastor warns, "It's impossible to stay anonymous here." Passing the peace lasts five minutes.

After the pastoral prayer, in which the gathered congregation shares joys and concerns, the congregation is invited into a time of meditation, during which a member of the congregation, a music professor at a nearby university, plays the cello. The preacher "preaches" from the center of the circle, but the sermon turns into a conversation with the parishioners about what we fear and how we keep ourselves defended, invulnerable. The conversation lasts twenty or thirty minutes, and parishioners share vulnerably about their deep fears and habits of defensiveness that preserves their illusion of invulnerability.

The service ends with the Lord's Supper. The pastor reminds the congregation that Christ instituted this meal, and he says the words of institution. Then he invites us to approach the table set with bread and wine (and grape juice) and serve another person at the table. As the congregation moves to the table a few people at a time, the cellist begins to play again. The time of Holy Communion transitions seamlessly into fellowship as people serve one another at the table and converse while eating a small piece of bread and drinking wine or grape juice. The service ends this way.

DISCUSS THIS:
HOW WOULD YOU DESCRIBE THE DIFFERENCES IN THESE THREE WORSHIP SERVICES? WHICH ONE MOST RESEMBLES THE WORSHIP IN YOUR CONGREGATION?

The service at Church One was "traditional"; Church Two, "contemporary." But what makes the service at Church Three different? The service can't be categorized by style, but style is not what sets it apart anyway.

MORE THAN STYLE

For years now, writers and thinkers have declared the end of the so-called worship wars, that struggle many congregations face as they battle over which "style" of worship to embrace—the options often offered in terms of "traditional," "contemporary," or "blended." But anyone who spends time within a congregation knows the war is far from over. And even a quick review of urban church websites shows that these categories are still dominant as churches try to help potential guests to understand what's going on inside.

But the persistence of the controversies in congregations and the ongoing marketing of our worship as contemporary, traditional, or something in between belies misunderstanding of worship's relationship to those outside the congregation and deep confusion about what worship really is. Few things are more important for the flourishing and faithfulness of urban congregations than to re-imagine worship as something much deeper than style.

How does the traditional/contemporary debate misunderstand worship's relationship with those outside of the congregation? Often, adding a contemporary service is employed as a growth strategy, thinking such a service will attract the people the congregation hasn't been able to reach with its current worship service. But what does this suggest about the people who might show up for the first time? *That they already know what worship is and what they want in worship.* These people are those who are switching churches, or who have left a church because the style of worship hasn't met their preferences. They are people who think worship should cater to their tastes and are shopping around. When we advertise a new contemporary service or put on our billboards the times of different styles of worship, we are inviting a particular kind of worshipper to join us: an informed consumer.

Such a strategy might get a few new people to show up, but it does little to help a congregation introduce non-Christians to life with God and in God's kingdom.

But perhaps even worse, this controversy, the obsession with style, and the belief that adding a service of a different style is the silver bullet to reverse decline (we've already said there are no silver bullets) shows a deep misunderstanding of worship. The purpose of worship is not and has never been to give people ignorant of the faith their first introduction to Christianity—to be the entry point into the People of God. Rather, worship aims to orient our lives—all that we are and do—in the direction of the God in whom we live and move and have our being. This purpose of worship can be fleshed out with three declarations.

WORSHIP IS THE PLACE WHERE WE ENACT OUR CORE HUMAN PURPOSE, THE END FOR WHICH WE EXIST—TO WORSHIP AND GLORIFY GOD.

Scientists define a human as *homo sapiens*—a thinking person. Theologians prefer *homo adorans*—a worshipping person. We are worshipping beings at the core; we can't not worship. That we worship the wrong things at the wrong time is the fundamental indicator of sin that marks our lives and the lives of our communities. Looking for a worship style that meets our preferences grows out of this disorder.

In worship we have our lives reordered and reoriented. The word *orient* means "east." It was traditional in the building of cathedrals that the altar faced to the east—the direction of the rising sun. In the early church, those about to be baptized faced west—the direction of the setting sun, of coming darkness—and renounced the spiritual forces of wickedness. Then they turned to the east to confess their faith in Jesus Christ. This ritual of baptism is a metaphor for all worship.

All worship should be a kind of reorientation. Our disordered worship is given its true order as our lives are turned toward the great mystery of the Triune God's love for us.

WORSHIP IS THE PLACE WHERE WE HAVE OUR VISION TRAINED TO SEE THE SIGNS OF GOD'S IN-BREAKING KINGDOM.

If a vision of God's kingdom is the landscape in which urban congregations begin to understand their lives, then we need ongoing training in recognizing and understanding that kingdom. But it's an upside-down kingdom, a surprising kingdom, the kingdom of a God whose thoughts are not our thoughts and whose ways are not our ways. The nature of the kingdom is seen supremely in the cross, in Christ's countercultural humility and sacrifice. Christ crucified appears to the world as a stumbling block and foolishness, but Christians believe him to be God's power and God's wisdom (see 1 Cor 1:24). So God's power is seen in the abandonment and suffering of the cross. These aren't realities that disoriented lives are able to see and respond to. It's in worship that we learn how to attend to and respond to this real though hidden kingdom, present among us and through us, in praise, gratitude, and service.

My (Roger's) six-year-old daughter used to love *I Spy* books filled with those complicated pictures with hidden images in them. But after you read these books for a few years, you get better at it. You begin to understand the mind of the maker of the puzzle and can more easily find the hidden items. Worship is where the hiddenness, humility, and countercultural ways of the kingdom show up—they are put front and center as the new orienting principle of our lives, so we are better at seeing and living these kingdom ways as we go about the rest of our days.

WORSHIP IS THE PLACE WHERE THE COMMUNITY REMEMBERS ITS IDENTITY AS GOD'S CALLED, GATHERED, AND SENT PEOPLE.

Ephesians 2 makes clear that God is creating a new humanity in the world, where the scattered, divisive, and violent ways of humanity are healed. It's in worship, when we are gathered and celebrating around the table of the one whose death and resurrection makes this people possible and whose ascension marks him as this body's living head, that we discover who we are. We remember in worship that we, as church, are a sign and foretaste of God's kingdom: in our life together the world is meant to see its ultimate purpose and destiny.

In other words, in worship we are re-membered. One way of looking at the brokenness of sin is to say that human unity is dismembered, broken apart. When we gather to worship, hearing again the story of our baptism, celebrating our union with the risen Lord around his table, we are re-membered, and we discover again our identity and purpose, our place in God's life and mission.

Worship obsessed with matching a particular style to people's shallow preferences does none of these things. In fact, it does just the opposite: it reinforces the disorder of lives that believe their own preferences are at the center. Our everyday lives, bombarded as they are by the promises of mass marketing that we should have what we want and that the solutions to our problems are a credit card swipe away, do not need to be reinforced by a view of worship that takes its place in the pantheon of consumer gods.

And *that's* what's wrong with the worship services at Church One and Church Two above—the ones that look "traditional" and "contemporary." There is more that unites them than divides them. On the surface they look very different—they have differing styles—but their deep logic is the same: the people up front, mostly the clergy, perform a show to be passively consumed by those in the hard pews or the padded seats. And what brings someone to one rather than another is often a similar logic: whichever meets our stylistic preferences.

While there's a slim chance urban congregations might increase worship attendance with a new style of worship, as long as they continue to think that nailing the right style to attract new worshippers is the answer, they won't be moving toward flourishing in their faithfulness to God's kingdom.

THE WORSHIP ALTERNATIVE

Church Three above is different. It followed what some would call a "traditional" order of liturgy, though there was no organ playing, and the clergy were not wearing robes. But there's also no way to call this a "blended" service, singing some music accompanied by the organ and other music with piano and drums in the background. Rather, the service was intentionally *formative*—and to have worship that is formative, worship that does the three things listed above, requires considerations that go beyond style.

Anthony Robinson, who pastored a large United Church of Christ in downtown Seattle as it underwent transformative changes, argues that the trouble with many mainline worship services is that they are no longer about God. They are about our own human projects and satisfying perceived human wants. He contends that churches facing the kind of adaptive challenges we've been writing about need to stop worrying so much about style and begin to ask to what extent our worship is theocentric, directing us toward the God whose self-sacrificial love has brought us into this place to begin with.[1] He writes that his urban congregation started asking different questions about worship:

> The questions we ask, now, as we leave the theater of worship are different. They are not first of all, "Was I pleased?" "Was I comfortable?" "Were my needs met?" Rather, we ask, "Did I worship—did we worship—God?" "Was God present?" "Was the Holy Spirit at work?" "Was God rightly praised?"[2]

TRY THIS:
LOOK BACK AT FOUR RECENT WORSHIP BULLETINS OR ORDERS OF WORSHIP FOR YOUR CHURCH. AS YOU GO THROUGH THEM, ASK: WHEN IN OUR WORSHIP WERE WE FOCUSED ON GOD? WHEN WAS THE HOLY SPIRIT AT WORK? WAS GOD RIGHTLY PRAISED? HOW WERE LIVES CHANGED?

These are crucial questions that urban congregations seeking renewal need to ask, questions more foundational than the worn-out questions about what style of worship people want.

But there are other questions as well. Once we have determined whether God is the center of our worship, and sought to put God back in the center, we need to talk about how we worship. Many times we focus on questions of style because we don't know what other questions to ask. Given the multiple and changing cultures of many urban centers, urban congregations seeking faithful renewal in worship need to ask three other questions.

IS OUR WORSHIP DEEPLY CONTEXTUAL?

This question matters because it is the alternative to the style question. While the gospel challenges any consumerist approach to worship that evaluates worship based on shallow, changing preferences, the gospel has always been enculturated, contextual. It's always embodied and expressed in the culture in which it seeks to take root. In fact, there's no "pure," non-contextual embodiment of Christianity. Attempts to improve worship import music, language, and other forms of expression from another congregation—perhaps a large, successful congregation—because of the perception that "if it worked there, it will work here," but too often the imported way of expressing the faith doesn't "fit."

DISCUSS THIS:
HOW DOES YOUR WORSHIP MIRROR THE CULTURAL EXPRESSIONS FOUND IN YOUR COMMUNITY OR NEIGHBORHOOD?

When my wife and I (Roger) were pastoring a rural congregation in North Carolina, we recognized that a rural culture is more likely to be an oral and aural culture—valuing the telling and hearing of stories—than it is to value the written word.[3] And so we changed the worship in this congregation so that it had more call-and-response aspects and singing of choruses that didn't need to be read. Ironically, this meant that we sang more praise music with simple choruses—a style of music many thought they wouldn't like, but which fit the cultural habits of the place. In my preaching, I almost never quoted books or talked about what I was reading. This was a contrast from when I pastored a church a mile from Duke University where the culture of that congregation valued learning and literacy.

The challenge with city churches is that many cultures are represented within the city and potentially within the congregation; worship that rural congregations might feel is too eclectic might seem very appropriate in an urban setting with a variety of cultural expressions.

Those planning and leading worship can't pay too much attention to what ways worship is being expressed through the language, images, idioms, and other embodiments of the culture of the congregation and the city in which it lives.

IS OUR WORSHIP DEEPLY VISUAL?

There is one cultural phenomenon facing the vast majority of congregations, but especially urban ones: the re-assurgency of the image. Walk through any city center and you will be overwhelmed with the visual display—its immediacy, power, and brilliance. Iconic images of Times Square indicate the power of the visual. In interpersonal communication, our language is supplemented by emoticons. Christianity has always known the power of the image. Confessing that humans are created in God's image, and that in Jesus we see the restored image of God, Christians have long sought to express their faith visually, though not without controversy. Eastern Orthodox Christians, who believe God's presence is mediated through icons, had to fight against the iconoclasts who opposed making these visual representations. Medieval Catholics told the story of the faith through the resplendent windows in their cathedrals and sanctuaries.

The Reformation, with its emphasis on the words of scripture, ushered in an era of visually sterile churches. But we ignore the power of image to our peril. Worship that is forming people who can see God's kingdom will learn to use images to shape the imaginations of people present. Technology allows the display of images on screens during worship; changes in the weekly bulletin can feature art; attentiveness to decoration in a place of worship can evoke mood and help the meaning of worship dwell more deeply in worshipers. Not to mention, we can learn from Eastern Orthodoxy and Catholicism, whose use of icons, images, statues, and candles doesn't rely on modern technology but is nonetheless deeply evocative of the holy.

IS OUR WORSHIP DEEPLY PARTICIPATORY?

This might be the most important question, one that encompasses the previous two, because when worship expresses the culture of the worshippers, they are more deeply engaged in worship. And, as Shane Hipps noted, "Images initially make us *feel* rather than *think*,"[4] and this image-rich worship speaks to a part of the human person other than the rational part. These questions invite us to think about participation:

- Does our worship invite people to bring, offer, and engage their whole selves in worship—body, mind, and heart?

- Are those gathered for worship actively involved, and are all their senses engaged?

- Do they get to touch the water, gaze upon the icons, approach the altar, adopt appropriate postures for prayer, connect physically with their neighbors?

- Or do they sit and observe while the clergy perform the acts of worship?

The job of worship leaders is not to be the center of attention but to facilitate the participatory action of those gathered—the very people whose work is to worship.

In this matter, worship planners and leaders should adapt to their contexts. Begin by asking about the senses and the body. In what ways are all five senses of the worshippers engaged in a worship service? We have worshipped in places where it would have made no difference if we had shown up as disembodied minds. But humans don't just think; we experience the world like the animals we are—through our skin, noses, eyes, ears, and mouths.

Worship that forms us in the way of Christ won't focus on ideas alone but will engage all the senses, the whole person.

To address the senses we consider our bodies. Worship doesn't need to feel like a gymnastics class to allow worshippers to be aware of how they are offering their bodies in worship. The simple invitation for worshippers to place their hands palms-up on their thighs during the pastoral prayer can form in them the understanding that prayer isn't just about asking God for things, it's also about being available to God's presence in that moment. Such simple transformations like an invitation to kneel or stand, occasional opportunities to move about the sanctuary, or the freedom to move with the music can allow worship to shape whole lives and not just minds.

The Apostle Paul instructs us to "let the same mind be in you that was in Christ Jesus" (Phil 2:5), but that way of translating the Greek seems too intellectual. That kind of formation focuses too much on ideas alone. New Testament scholar Stephen Fowl suggests that a better translation, one that gets the full flavor of the Greek, might be, "Let this be your pattern of thinking, acting, and feeling, which was also displayed in Christ Jesus."[5] In other words, we should be formed holistically as disciples.

Worship should help this happen. God-centered worship that is contextual, image-rich, and deeply participatory will facilitate this transformation.

HOMEGROWN WORSHIP

In worship we present our bodies to God. We also present our gifts. Many of us are used to presenting gifts during the offertory, when we are invited to "give back to God our tithes and our offerings." At the offering we are thinking about our gifts of money.

But the gifts of people sitting in the pews or the seats on Sunday mornings are much more varied than financial gifts alone. They are musicians, artists, decorators, computer programmers, storytellers, comedians, writers—the gifts are endless. Urban environments are centers of creativity, but how often do these people find places in our churches to offer these gifts to God? By not inviting individuals to offer gifts other than money, we are contributing to keeping their lights under a basket.

Tour any major city and you will find vacant church buildings that are turned into art museums, concert venues, and restaurants. No longer churches, a full range of God-given gifts are being expressed in these spaces. What we want to know is this: can these offerings of gifts happen *before* the church is closed? Can our worship be created from the ground up—using the gifts of the people in the congregation and the city?

It's not uncommon for churches to allow their spaces to be used as venues for the arts outside of worship, and this is a good start. But what about *in* worship? Maybe rather than buying the rights to sing and project on a screen the lyrics to songs every other church is singing, we should find the poets and composers in our congregations and allow them to write hymns and choruses for worship. Elements of the liturgy—the call to worship, opening prayers, prayers of confessions, and other elements—can be written by members of the congregation. In worship at one urban church service, a prayer of confession was a spoken-word poetry piece. A young woman who performs at poetry slams on Saturday nights in the city used her gifts to lead people in confession during worship. Those entering worship can be greeted by original art in the narthex, and the worship space itself can be decorated using the gifts and imaginations of those who are part of the worshipping community.

The beginning step is to list people and their gifts within the congregation. Are there musicians, composers, writers, actors, visual artists and graphic designers, videographers, poets, and dancers? Next, list the elements of a worship service these people could help create. Don't be afraid to think outside of the box. There's no better way to have appropriately contextual and deeply participatory worship than to have worshippers themselves use their gifts to create the elements of worship.

TRY THIS:
LIST THE ARTISTS AND CULTURE-MAKERS IN YOUR CONGREGATION, THEN BEGIN TO IMAGINE WAYS THEY COULD BE INVITED TO CONTRIBUTE TO WORSHIP.

Some people might think to stop here, but we suggest taking it a step further. Don't look only within the congregation. Look around the city and find the culture-makers within the wider community. What are they doing and creating that can find a place in Christian worship? Can they be commissioned to paint, write, or compose? These fresh creative voices can help us to renew worship from the ground up.

ONE MORE CHURCH

Open Door Church, a church we wrote about at the end of chapter 2, invited me (Roger) to preach for a month while the lead pastor was on sabbatical. I wanted to have a sense for their worship before preaching for them so I joined this young, urban congregation one Sunday morning. The first thing I noticed was an icon of the Holy Trinity projected onto a wall above the communion table. The seats were arranged in three sections facing one another. This arrangement increased the visual power of worship, for rather than staring at the backs of heads, the worshippers could see the faces of others in the space. The faces I saw were intergenerational and multiracial. In the middle was the communion table, which was set with the communion elements and a bowl of water. The call to worship and prayer of confession were both read responsively from words projected onto a wall, the congregation alternating reading between the left and right halves.

It was clear that the prayers, both the ones spoken by the worship leaders and the ones spoken in unison, were written for that congregation—there was nothing generic about them. During a baptism, along with the denomination's prescribed baptismal vows, the one being baptized was asked if she would uphold the core practices of the congregation. After the baptism the whole congregation was invited to come forward and touch the water as a way of remembering their own baptisms and renewing their baptismal vows.

The sermon focused on the prophet Jeremiah's injunction in Jeremiah 29:7 to "promote the welfare of the city," especially by praying for it. At the end of the sermon, the pastor invited us to turn to a neighbor and name two or three ways we want to pray for our city. The pastor acknowledged that some people are uncomfortable praying aloud in front of others, so after this sharing we were invited into three minutes of silence in which to pray for those aspects of the city we mentioned. A couple of minutes of murmuring and conversing melded into silence as the congregation joined in prayer for the city. Not only was this a way of inviting participation by asking the congregation to pray, this exercise engaged the sense of sound in an unusual way—rarely do we hear either the voices of people chatting or extended silence in worship.

This church celebrates Holy Communion each Sunday, realizing that the Eucharist is the crucial act in which we are formed as Christians; it is also the act that engages most fully the whole person. The communion liturgy invites singing, walking, seeing, smelling, touching, and eating. At the table where we remember Christ's giving his whole self for the world and experience Christ's ongoing presence with us, we are invited to present our whole selves—body and soul—to Christ and to receive his pardoning and transforming grace.

Some church growth experts, trained in the techniques of the 1980s and 1990s might have objected to some of the practices, such as having the worshippers divide into pairs and talk, since this might be intimidating to an introvert or someone there for the first time. But when we stop insisting that worship is measured by growth in the crowds, and start imaging worship as the formation of people and communities in the ways of the kingdom, this urban congregation is one many others can learn from.

BETTER TOGETHER: SERVING TOGETHER AS PASTOR, STAFF, AND LAITY

SOMETHING'S NOT RIGHT

Two anecdotes illustrate twin temptations of leadership: the temptation to do all the work yourself and the temptation to delegate it all to others.

When my wife and I (Roger) were appointed to lead Duke Memorial, we had an initial meeting with the personnel committee. The committee was asked to share with us what they were excited about at the church, but also to share something that needed attention, something that needed to be "fixed." One man on the committee told us pointedly: "We need you to do something about adult Sunday school." Then he proceeded to share with us the dismal statistics of decline in adult Sunday school attendance, suggesting that insufficient staff attention might have something to do with the decline.

It was no surprise to me that a declining urban congregation would be facing challenges in adult Sunday school. If it had become increasingly hard to get adults to attend worship, how much harder must it have been to get them to come to a class for the hour before worship? And with this announcement of the problem, I faced my first leadership temptation—a ubiquitous one for most pastors—before I'd even moved into my office: fix it myself. I was being invited to apply what expertise I had (or fake it if I didn't have expertise) to "fix" the adult Sunday school—start more classes, grow the old ones, show them I know how to lead. But something in me said that was not the right approach.

The other temptation woos a leader in the opposite direction: stay uninvolved, hands off.

As much as I admire the ministry and scholarship of Eugene Peterson (I routinely assign his books in my ministry classes), one passage in his memoir *The Pastor* didn't sit right with me when I read it the first time. He tells about how the euphoria of starting and growing a church began to wane, and he nearly suffered burnout. The wake-up call came to him when one evening as he was leaving his house for a church meeting his five-year-old daughter said to him, "This is the twenty-seventh night in a row you have had a meeting."[1] Here's how he describes the impact that statement had on him: "In the seven-minute walk to the church on the way to the meeting I made a decision. If succeeding as a pastor meant failing as a parent, I was already a failed pastor. I would resign that very night."[2] Which he did.

But the lay leaders of the congregation, those present at the meeting, didn't accept his resignation. Instead they worked with him to make an arrangement that would allow him to focus on those things he felt were the proper work of a pastor—preaching, teaching, praying, providing spiritual direction—and they would take care of the business of the church. The leaders assured him that their own professions and careers had given them the experience they needed to care for the administrative aspects of church life. From that point on he would go to no committee meetings. He would have to learn to trust the leaders.[3]

Is the wisest course of action, when a leader is doing too much and facing burnout, to simply abandon certain aspects of ministry and hand them over? Something didn't seem right about this course of action. Surely there is faithful territory between fixing problems, running a church by oneself, and handing the work over completely.

Yes, there is, and living in this territory is the sweet spot for urban congregations seeking renewal.

DISCUSS THIS:
HOW DO YOU REACT TO THESE TWO ANECDOTES?
HOW DO YOU THINK THESE SITUATIONS SHOULD BE HANDLED?

THE CHALLENGE—WHY PARTNERSHIP IS NECESSARY

In his book *Becoming a Leader Is Becoming Yourself*, Russ Moxley quotes John Ryan, the president of the Center for Creative Leadership: "We focus more on making sure the days of superman are over. We have a VUCA world: volatility, uncertainty, complexity, ambiguity... [Y]ou are only going to handle this complexity if you get the best from everybody."[4]

This quotation is just another way of putting what we've been saying all along: when organizations are in situations of confusion, change, and decline they often search for expert solutions, professional fixes, leaders who have the knowledge and experience to solve problems, dispel confusion, and get things back on track. That's what the member of the personnel committee wanted from my wife and me—five easy steps out of our malaise (and I was almost foolish enough to think we could give it).

But adult Sunday school is a perfect example of a problem for which there is no single authoritative solution. Leaders who try to "fix it" on their own will only find themselves facing burnout and failure.

Broad social trends make looking to the leader for expert solutions, especially for urban congregations, a less than ideal option. Leadership theorist and historian Barbara Kellerman notes that twenty-first-century culture is facing the "end of leadership."[5] The twentieth century, she argues, saw a decreased appreciation for the authority and power of leaders with an accompanying rise in the power of so-called followers. In every sector of society and across organizations, people with little power have been "taking on the powerful, demanding, finally, greater equity."[6] Along with the relative rise of followers, Kellerman sees a decrease in the willingness of those in organizations to defer to leaders—what she calls a shift in "patterns of dominance and deference."[7] The upshot of her research is a warning to leaders: even in situations when it seems like an organization wants authoritative expertise, don't assume you have the power and that the "followers" will defer to it.

These trends are crucial for urban congregations to understand. While some segments of society, like rural areas, might be lagging behind the broader cultural shifts Kellerman is highlighting, cities will be at the front of those shifts. City-dwellers and urban professionals will be increasingly used to working in flat-organizations, where everyone's creativity, expertise, and ingenuity contributes to a company's thriving, and where shifts in technology continue to level the playing field as a leader's authoritative knowledge is diminished by everyone having access to information.[8] The implication for the church is this: While older, more established members may be satisfied with a pastor's authoritative expertise if that expertise promises to bring a return to the church's former glory, younger members and newer attendees may not be satisfied in a church where the pastors and staff call the shots and do the work without engaging the knowledge, creativity, and gifts of the wider congregation.

Neither of the options presented in the first section of this chapter—doing the work yourself or handing it all over—are sufficient for the complex territory urban congregations need to inhabit. When churches face challenges for which there are no cookie-cutter solutions, and when cultural change demands that leaders be more collaborative—honoring the gifts and resources of "followers"—congregations are going to have to become learning communities where pastors, staff, and laity together learn how to share leadership, to discern together, and to co-create with God a future worthy of God's kingdom.

Ron Heifetz and Martin Linsky give us language to understand this territory between "do the work yourself" and "hand the work over." They say that in situations of adaptive change, leaders need to learn to "give the work back" to the people.[9] By this they do *not* mean that leaders simply hand it over and remain uninvolved, washing their hands of the matter, Pilate-like. Rather they argue that giving the work back to the people acknowledges that when organizations face adaptive challenges, the *whole* organization needs to learn, grow, develop new habits, and let go of old expectations. And this work of learning to adapt is work the leader can't do for the people. On the other hand, it's often work the people don't want to do (because this kind of change always means giving something up) and work many people don't know how to do (because they haven't ever done it before). And so the leader, far from handing the work over completely, stays intimately involved in the adaptive learning and work, mostly by creating the space within which the organization can do the work it needs to do and by pacing the work of learning and adapting so that it gets done.[10]

Of course, these insights from secular leadership experts only point us back to the key biblical word that helps a congregation make sense of the relationship between a church's staff and laity: *equipping*—a word that must be recovered if congregations are going to learn, grow, and thrive together.

RELEARNING THE BIBLICAL MODEL

If pastoral leaders and staff learn to give the work back to the people, the work begins by recovering a biblical understanding of a leader's role to "equip God's people for the work of serving" (Eph 4:12). For many pastors and staff, this will mean learning a way of ministry we weren't taught in seminary.

Many seminary curricula are still designed for a church that no longer exists, the church of Christendom that assumed the role of a pastoral leader was to adequately perform religious duties. So seminary curricula are designed to teach leaders how to do the work of ministry rather than equipping others for the work of service. A course in preaching teaches prospective pastors how to exegete a biblical text and write and deliver a faithful sermon; it does *not* teach them how to identify, encourage, and equip others in the congregation who might have a gift for interpreting and teaching God's word. A course in pastoral care teaches prospective pastors how to be with the grieving and the dying as a witness to Christ's presence; it does not teach them how to discover individuals in the congregation with gifts for caregiving, train them, and deploy them so that the congregation learns to be pastoral caregivers for one another. In this case, seminary trains in the doctrine of what one friend of ours has called *sola Pastora*—the doctrine (heresy, really) that says only a visit by the pastor "counts" as pastoral care.[11]

Most seminary graduates have very little training in helping congregations and their members discover and use the gifts God has given them to faithfully live in God's kingdom, to witness to Christ, and to help God's people flourish as a community, despite the fact that this is the clear biblical mandate for leaders:

> [God] gave some apostles, some prophets, some evangelists, and some pastors and teachers. His purpose was to equip God's people for the work of serving and building up the body of Christ until we all reach the unity of faith and knowledge of God's Son. God's goal is for us to become mature adults—to be fully grown, measured by the standard of the fullness of Christ (Eph 4:11-13).

This biblical injunction for leaders to focus on equipping is based on another biblical assumption: that all baptized Christians possess gifts that need to be discovered, used, and honed, for the gifts of the Spirit are the particularization of the Spirit's work in each individual life. And the church needs them all, working together (see 1 Cor 12). For many people this will be basic knowledge—something they've heard before. But many churches in decline have never moved from a knowledge of the universal giftedness of all the baptized and of the leaders' role to equip to putting this knowledge into practice. But given the adaptive challenges so many congregations face, there's no better time to start than now.

While we critiqued Bill Hybels of Willow Creek Community Church for a too leader-centered understanding of vision (see chapter 2), we applaud Willow Creek and urge other congregations to learn from their commitment to being a church that equips. Don Cousins, who was a founding leader of Willow Creek, describes their commitment to moving the people of the church from being "consumers" to being "contributors."[12] This strategy mitigates some concern that Willow Creek is too consumer-oriented to worship and ministry. Cousins says most churches embody a model of ministry in which the staff serves, the congregation is served, and the world is ignored; he calls this "organizational heresy."[13] For many congregations used to paying religious professionals (pastors and staff) to do the work of ministry, moving to a model like the one Cousins suggests—in which pastors and staff lead by equipping, so that the congregation itself becomes a body of servants, and the world is served—will itself be an adaptive change, a new way of thinking about and living into shared ministry.

DISCUSS THIS:
HOW DO YOU UNDERSTAND THE MINISTRY OF EQUIPPING?
DO YOU KNOW YOUR GIFTS AND HOW YOU ARE USING THEM?
DOES YOUR CONGREGATION HAVE A CONSUMER CULTURE
OR AN EXPECTATION FOR PEOPLE TO CONTRIBUTE?

FIVE (NOT-SO-EASY) STEPS TOWARD EQUIPPING

For churches that want to make this shift—for leaders who want to "give the work back" in a biblically faithful way, and for congregation members who long to be partners with pastors and staff in doing the work of ministry—we have five suggestions.

FIRST, TEACH CURRENT STAFF, LEADERS, AND THE WIDER CONGREGATION TO UNDERSTAND THE VALUE OF EQUIPPING.

This understanding is relevant especially for pastors who are leading staff used to doing the work themselves: Teach! Don't waste an opportunity to share a vision of the pastors and staff as equippers. Repeat it again and again: every baptized Christian has gifts of the Spirit; no gifts are more important than others; the church will flourish and God's world will be served when people discover and use their gifts (that is, when they let the Holy Spirit particularize the Spirit's ministry through them); and leaders have the role of helping the baptized discern and hone those gifts. In other words: teach over and over Ephesians 4, 1 Corinthians 12, and the meaning of Christian baptism.

TRY THIS:
BRAINSTORM TOGETHER A FOUR-WEEK WORSHIP SERIES ON EQUIPPING. WHAT TEXTS WOULD THE SERMONS BE BASED ON? WHO WOULD GIVE TESTIMONIES? HOW WOULD YOU INVITE PEOPLE TO RESPOND?

SECOND, COACH CURRENT STAFF TO BE EQUIPPERS.

After Ginger and I (Roger) became the pastors of Duke Memorial, I don't think a staff meeting went by in which we didn't talk about the importance of the staff being equippers. And they had many questions, because at that point the staff was functioning along the less biblical but more traditional model: they were doing much of the work of ministry—teaching classes, visiting the sick, setting up for events, and generally doing too much work themselves. So our coaching took the form of reminding them that the temptation to simply do it yourself is strong; after all, that means you keep control and get things done the "right" way. Equipping others—giving the work back—means developing the capacity to *not* have things your way all the time and to be flexible and patient. We also reminded them that equipping doesn't save time; it's just as hard or harder than doing the work yourself. We required staff to bring to staff meetings a list of people they were actively equipping, people in whom they were investing their time and energy to help them realize their gifts and put them to work. Then we encouraged them to do one important thing: Ask for specific feedback from the people they were equipping, especially using the question, "What do you need from me to do this ministry well?"

DISCUSS THIS:
WHEN HAVE YOU ASKED OR BEEN ASKED THIS QUESTION, "WHAT DO YOU NEED FROM ME?" WHAT DIFFERENCE DID IT MAKE?

This is an important question because what a staff person believes is giving someone space to "figure things out" or the freedom to do something their way can be perceived as abandonment: *They told me I had this gift, they encouraged me in this new ministry, and then they abandoned me!* Staff members need to invite laypeople to be explicit with them about what kind of equipping is most helpful to them.

THIRD, HIRE STAFF MEMBERS WHO HAVE A PASSION FOR AND TRACK RECORD OF EQUIPPING.

When it's time to hire a new staff person, this is an excellent time to revise a job description, making explicit the expectation that new staff member will be committed to equipping. Hiring a minister of visitation, for instance? Make it clear that the congregation doesn't expect this person to do all the visiting; rather, most of his or her efforts should be in creating teams of visitors—laypeople who have the gift of listening, of presence, who can minister to the homebound, the sick, and the dying. The staff minister can equip people by telling them, "I see in you gifts for this ministry"; by offering training sessions and accompanying new visitation ministers on their visits; by convening teams to share with one another what they are learning as they visit and to support one another when the ministry is difficult. Ask an applicant for the job: If you had a room of twenty people who need visits and another room of twenty people who need to be equipped to make visits, which room would you rather enter?[14] Let the same mindset guide your hiring for other staff positions as well.

FOURTH, DEVELOP WAYS FOR PEOPLE TO EXPLORE AND IDENTIFY THEIR SPIRITUAL GIFTS.

There are many ways to go about this—and we don't recommend a certain process. What we want to emphasize is that one of the chief ministries of a congregation is providing pathways for people to explore spiritual gifts, identify their own, and begin to claim a ministry. Some churches will adopt very simple spiritual gifts inventories. These are often short and not completely adequate but can be better than nothing, especially in getting the ball rolling. We knew an adult discipleship minister once who firmly (and probably rightly) believed that people best identify their gifts when they participate in community with others over several months, so that the community can name what gifts they see in each member. Many churches use an in-depth Bible study such as *Covenant* (www.covenantbiblestudy.com) or *Disciple* (www.adult biblestudies.com), in which the participants spend one hundred or more minutes together each week for 24 or 34 weeks with a retreat at the end. During the retreat, the participants name the spiritual gifts they have seen in each other. We have seen people claim and begin to use their gifts coming out of these retreats in life-transforming and community-building ways.

DISCUSS THIS:
HOW IS YOUR CONGREGATION INTENTIONAL ABOUT HELPING PEOPLE EXPLORE, IDENTIFY, DEVELOP, AND USE THEIR GIFTS? HOW CAN YOU IMPROVE?

FIFTH, TELL STORIES.

We've already said the pastor should be a storyteller. And that doesn't change; not only does the pastor need to take every opportunity to tell stories about when she has seen the wider kingdom vision being lived and embodied, she also needs to tell stories about when she has seen members of the church discovering and using their gifts in service and leadership. But it's not only the pastor's job. Congregations need to find ways to communicate the significance of staff who equip and laypeople who discover and use their gifts. When new members join the congregation, give them a chance to say how they plan to use the gifts they have discovered and honed through the new member process; let testimonies in worship focus on how the Holy Spirit is making particular the Spirit's ministry in people's lives; give staff members a chance—in worship, at meetings, through newsletters, on social media—to narrate how they are helping people in their ministry areas flourish in gift-based ministry. The more stories people hear, the more their own longing to be active participants in the leadership and ministry of the congregation—that is, active participants in the mission of God in that place—will grow.

There are no *easy* steps to make an adaptive change, and for most congregations giving the work back to the people—developing a culture of shared ministry and leadership based on the giftedness of every believer—will be an adaptive change. But the five not-so-easy steps above can help move the needle in the right direction.

Here are some brief questions it might be helpful to use with staff and laypeople to see the degree to which equipping ministry is happening in your congregation:

FOR PASTORS AND STAFF

- Can you list five to ten people whom you are equipping—in whom you are investing your time and energy as they develop their gifts for leadership and ministry?

- Can you describe how you are equipping them? If you asked these people how you are equipping them, what would they say?

- What do you do when you find a certain ministry is just easier when you show up and do it yourself? What is your natural reaction to this situation?

- Looking back over the last couple of years, can you describe the fruit of the ministry of those people you have helped to discover and use their gifts?

FOR LAYPEOPLE

- Are there staff in your church currently helping you to discover and use your gifts for leadership and ministry? How are they helping you?

- Do you know what your spiritual gifts are?

- How do you find yourself using your gifts in daily life— in the home, at work, at church?

- Looking back over the last couple of years, can you describe the fruit you've seen coming from your own commitment to using your gifts for leadership and ministry?

TRY THIS:
GATHER A GROUP OF STAFF PEOPLE AND LAYPEOPLE AND HAVE THEM SHARE THEIR ANSWERS TO THESE QUESTIONS. AT THE END, HAVE A CONVERSATION ABOUT WHAT YOU HAVE LEARNED ABOUT EQUIPPING PEOPLE FOR GIFT-BASED MINISTRY IN YOUR CONGREGATION.

GIVING IT A SHOT

At Duke Memorial, I (Roger) didn't step in and fix the adult Sunday school problem. I tried to listen beneath the words. Though decline in adult Sunday school was the "presenting issue," I suspected there was a deeper, adaptive problem, one very common in established, mainline congregations (not just urban ones): we didn't know how to be intentional about adult Christian formation. Besides Sunday school (which was dwindling), we didn't know how to help adults grow in lives of prayer, faith, and service. It's very difficult for equipping to happen in the absence of intentional adult formation. And I knew this was something we would have to work *together* to fix; this problem was not mine alone to solve.

So after about a year, I put two teams together. I found people with gifts for leadership and asked them if they would lead study teams. One team focused on ways to improve and make more robust, faithful, and effective the program of adult Sunday school. I worked with that leader to find the right people for this team. They worked for months, holding focus groups with the congregation, studying other congregations, reading books, and getting feedback. Their discoveries weren't surprising. Rather than suggest we needed a staff person to do more of the adult Sunday school work, they discovered that adult teachers didn't feel sufficiently equipped to lead, teach, organize, and choose curriculum; they felt abandoned. This was useful information because it helped us as we were putting a job description together for a new minister of adult discipleship to realize that a key capacity for anyone in this staff position was being available to the leaders of adult Sunday school for coaching and support, while helping to identify and support new leaders with the gifts for leading groups.

The other group was designed to study what we could do to support adult formation at times other than the Sunday school hour. This team also led focus groups, looked at what other churches were doing, read books, and spent time in prayer and discernment, eventually deciding that, along with adult Sunday school, we needed seasonal, short-term small groups that could help folks in the congregation connect to one another, practice together the areas of ministry that made up our vision, grow in their faith, and help one another discover their spiritual gifts.

This process was effective because:

1. It was collaborative, team-based work from the beginning. The people of the church took the ball and ran with it.

2. The work showed how we were inadequately equipping current leaders for the roles they were in, and we needed to do a better job of that.

3. Each team came up with ideas that were aimed at better helping people discover and use their gifts for ministry as we together tried to live into the vision of the church.

4. The work of these teams highlighted the fact that in hiring our next minister of adult discipleship, a passion and gift for equipping leaders to teach and guide small groups would be essential.

This kind of story, in any area of ministry, is possible anywhere when pastors and leaders decide not to "fix it" themselves but to share the work of ministry with others, as the culture of a congregation shifts in the direction of shared ministry and leadership based on the Holy Spirit's gifts to all the baptized.

Conclusion

THE ALTAR CALL: WHO'S WILLING TO COME FORWARD?

When I (Donna) first arrived at Mount Vernon Place, our ninety-seven-year-old chair of the personnel committee would never end a meeting without looking me straight in the eye and saying, "Donna, Mount Vernon Place is in the center of the city. Washington needs Mount Vernon Place, and Mount Vernon Place needs you. Don't you ever forget that you have the best job in Washington."

At the time, I thought Mabel was crazy. Did she have any idea how hard it was to swim against what felt like a sea of resistance? Did she understand how many of my peers and individuals younger than me had already given up on the church? Had she heard the comments offered by her fellow church members indicating how they were prepared to spend the endowment and close the doors of the church instead of pushing forward into new life?

Thankfully, Mabel's words filled my heart and spirit. When I was ready to give up, her constant encouragement and persistence convinced me that Washington did, in fact, need this church to not only stay alive but thrive. And I'm now convinced that every city needs thriving congregations with faithful disciples who are seeking to make a difference in their community.

Several people have said that Mount Vernon Place is like a new church since over 75 percent of our congregation has joined or come to the church in the last decade. Those words couldn't be further from the truth, however. Mount Vernon Place is alive today because a group of older adults were willing to let go of so much of what they knew and loved, including buildings they helped to build and traditions they cherished, in order to make space for God to do a new thing. And the same can happen in your community regardless of how many people you have to start with or what the average age of your congregation might be.

Both Mount Vernon Place and Duke Memorial are in very different places today than they were when we first walked through their doors as pastors. They know and love their neighbors. They consistently have new members who are growing in their love of God and neighbor. They have worship that is participatory, engaging, and formative. They strive for excellence. And they continue to imagine how to faithfully live in the landscape of God's kingdom of shalom. They are, by God's grace, bearing fruit when they could have easily continued to decline or even close.

We end the book with the same wish with which we started: if only turning around existing congregations could be done with a simple recipe, a one-size-fits-all approach. The recipe doesn't exist, and you shouldn't try to wear someone else's shoes or skinny jeans. But you can courageously move forward with an attitude of expectation, and we pray you have found helpful suggestions for how to take your next faithful step in leading change wherever you might be.

In chapter 1, you read about pruning. Cutting back is essential for any living thing to continue to grow. It is impossible to move forward without letting go of something. This step may be your most difficult one to take, but it's also the one that will most enable you to see what's truly important and where God is at work.

Chapter 2 offers you compelling reasons for why a clear vision isn't always adequate to the complex situations of declining urban congregations and the diverse and rapidly changing contexts in which they are located. You may never be able to state exactly where your congregation is headed, but you can constantly imagine and seek to live into the vision of the kind of people you feel called to be. Embrace the gift of fluidity and see adaptive challenges as a gift.

Chapter 3 is an invitation to open yourself as wide as possible to the journey. There is no way you can predict exactly what your congregation's future will hold and the strategy necessary for arriving in that place. What you can do is constantly be on the lookout for where God is at work and how you are being invited to faithfully respond and change as a result. Seize the opportunity to experiment, and discover delight in the gift of being surprised!

We've spent plenty of money on books that tell us how to win new people, making membership recruitment as easy as three simple steps. We have also been regularly tempted to grow our congregations as big as possible without paying attention to the depth of discipleship. Chapter 4 is an invitation to be with people, show up often, and discover that faithful mission and evangelism boil down to just that.

"Whatever you do, do it from the heart for the Lord and not for people," Paul encourages the Colossians (Col 3:23). We can't overestimate the importance of offering your best in all you do as congregations. Chapter 5 is a sincere request to embody excellence in all you say, create, publish, build, and do. God and God's people deserve our very best.

The temptation to entertain people through worship or provide a menu of styles from which to choose is real, especially when you feel a greater sense of desperation to grow for growth's sake. Chapter 6 reminds us that the purpose of worship is God. How can you passionately embrace your context while weaving the gifts of your community and the city through your liturgy?

Many of us love a challenge, and a majority of people who embrace challenges approach them with the confidence that they can fix just about anything. But your role as pastors and lay leaders in the urban church is not to fix anything on your own. Rather, you are encouraged to collaborate in ways that allow numerous people to use their gifts. Chapter 7 offers a fresh look at equipping the saints in hopes that you can transform your congregation from consumers to contributors.

While we suggested that the first step you take is to prune and let go, we pray you can embrace these seven conversations as keepsakes. Even more so, we pray you will discover something to hold onto in each chapter.

I recently had a conversation with a pastor who was being recruited by two different congregations who wanted to have her as their next pastor. When I asked her why she felt led to choose one over the other, she shared how one congregation's leadership did not speak with enough desperation. "They were not desperate enough to grow again."

Many of our congregations are declining, but few are desperate enough to do what it takes to grow and make a vital difference in the community again. Oxford Dictionaries defines desperation as "a state of despair, typically one which results in rash or extreme behaviour."[1] While we do not advocate that a congregation embody rash behavior, your final invitation is to embrace desperation and allow it to result in extreme behavior that is willing to let go, seize the adventure, and try new things.

Enjoy the journey. We would not trade ours for anything.

HOSTING RENEWAL CONVERSATIONS: A GUIDE TO GETTING STARTED

Throughout this book we've resisted the impulse to give easy answers (because there are none). Local contexts differ, as well as the particular challenges in each congregation. What's key is that each congregation have the space to look honestly at their own situation and begin to discern how God is leading them forward. We believe this book can be a part of that process. So rather than giving easy answers, we offer below a brief and flexible guide to using this book in a congregation that allows participants to have the conversations it needs to have, while at the same time knowing that conversation alone doesn't bring renewal. This guide to hosting renewal conversations is aimed, in the end, at leading toward experimentation, trial, and risk—taking the next steps with God into an as yet unknown but exciting future.[1]

Issue invitations to the conversation. There are two ways to do this. The first is to prayerfully discern a small group of people who would serve as an initial conversation group. The other, a riskier but in the end more appealing option, is to issue a general invitation to the conversation to all people who are interested in investing their time and energy in following God to a place of flourishing ministry for the congregation. Important in this invitation is to express your own hopefulness about the future and to set out the expectations for participation, which should be high. Folks who can't make it to the gatherings or don't want to read the book or aren't willing to pray between gatherings needn't bother to attend. Be explicit about these expectations. Make it clear that these gatherings are not aimed at making decisions for the church; rather, they are spaces to discern our current reality and imagine with God a more hopeful future.

Set up the room. If a small group of people gather for the conversation, the room should be arranged so everyone can see each other and no one seems singled out, including the leader. If the group is large, make sure there are ways to break into groups of three or four. Select a room that is spacious, with high ceilings and plenty of light—preferably windows. When we have meetings in our churches, we pay too little attention to where we gather. A spacious, uncluttered environment can inspire spacious, uncluttered thinking. You can start modeling excellence in your meetings together through how you prepare the room, welcome people, and offer hospitality.

Reinforce the commitment and establish ground rules. At the first meeting, remind those present that this is a *high participation* gathering. It matters to show up on time and stay until the end (with the leader honoring an agreed upon ending time). Those participating should read and think about the chapter for discussion before coming. Some ground rules might include: Not interrupting others; speaking your truth and not someone else's;

letting others speak before anyone speaks a second time; paying attention and showing respect to anyone who is speaking; and praying for God's guidance between gatherings. We've found it helpful to encourage people, when they find themselves disagreeing with someone or getting angry at what someone said, to turn instead to wonder: "I wonder what brought this person to this point of view? I wonder why they are so passionate about this?" This act of "wondering" can help us to tune into a speaker, rather than into our own negative reactions and responses.[2]

Guide the conversation. Begin each conversation by dwelling in scripture. The leader should pick a passage of scripture that seems appropriate to the chapter being discussed at that meeting. Read through the scripture one time inviting those present to "listen for a word or phrase that captures your attention." After the reading, allow for a couple of minutes of silence and then a chance for those gathered to share the word or phrase without explanation or commentary. Then read the passage again, asking people to "listen for how this scripture might be speaking to our congregation." After the second reading, offer a couple minutes of silence, and then let people share in a small group what they heard. Reinforce that this is a time of sharing, not a time for conversation or debate.

Second, allow people to share their reactions to the chapter under discussion, reactions that go deeper than "I liked it" or "I didn't like it" or "I disagreed with it." Rather, encourage people to share where they felt excited while reading, or anxious, or angry, or confused. How we react to what we are reading can tell us a great deal about ourselves. Since no one's reaction can be wrong, this isn't a time for debate, argument, or correction but for honest sharing and open listening. Too many congregations lack this space, but without it we can be held captive to reactions and have difficulty moving forward.

Third, use the "Discuss This" and "Try This" exercises within each chapter to begin delving deeper into the content of each chapter and discovering how it relates to your congregational context. Be open, and see where the conversation goes from here.

Consider what's next. Invite people to keep lists of ideas or suggestions they heard mentioned during the conversation and at the end of the conversation share what was heard. Keep a list of these ideas and suggestions as you move through the book, as these ideas might be key places to begin discernment about next steps. The group can decide to go through the whole book, then return to the topic of each chapter to consider possible experiments within the congregation, or the group can spend a few months on each chapter, discerning and practicing next steps for each one before moving on. We recommend, however, reading the whole book first.

End with discerning questions. At the end of each meeting have some silence. Invite participants to let their minds roam through the memory of the conversation they just had, asking the Holy Spirit to reveal what is of significance. Then ask these questions:

- Where have we sensed God's Spirit leading us in this conversation? Where was there hope and energy?

- Where do we need God's guidance as we move forward in this area of church life?

- For what do we have to give thanks for our time together?

- Did an obvious next step emerge?

Someone should keep track of the answers to these questions, and at any time the group should consider pursuing further new possibilities—experiments and clear action steps—that seem to have energy and the Spirit's blesssing.

NOTES

INTRODUCTION

1. Frederick Buechner, *Now and Then: A Memoir of Vocation* (New York: HarperCollins, 1983), 31.

2. William Sloane Coffin, *Credo* (Louisville: Westminster John Knox, 2004), 140–41.

1. BEFORE THE GROWTH, THE PRUNING SHEARS

1. Ronald Heifetz, Alexander Grashow, and Marty Linsky, *The Practice of Adaptive Leadership* (Boston: Harvard Business Press, 2009), 69.

2. "Grapes: Planting, Growing, and Harvesting Grapes," *The Old Farmer's Almanac*, www.almanac.com/plant/grapes.

3. "Pruning—A Special Case—Renovating Old Fruit Trees," *PennState Extension*, http://extension.psu.edu/plants/gardening /fphg/pome/pruning/pruning-a-special-case-renovating-old-fruit -trees.

4. Amy Butler, interview with the author, [June 22, 2016].

5. John P. Kotter, *Leading Change* (Boston: Harvard Business Review Press, 2009), 44.

6. Thomas Merton, *New Seeds of Contemplation* (New York: New Directions Books, 1961), 203.

7. www.edgehillcommunity.org.

8. www.edgehill.org.

9. Emily Askew, *Feasting on the Gospels*, vol. 2, *John*, ed. Cynthia A. Jarvis and E. Elizabeth Johnson (Louisville: Westminster John Knox, 2015), 172.

10. Roberto A. Ferdman, "This is a Terrible Sign for McDonald's," *Washington Post*, August 13, 2015, www.washingtonpost.com/news/wonk/wp/2015/08/13/mcdonalds-is-shrinking/.

2. DESTINATION OR JOURNEY?

1. Wyatt T. Dixon, *Ninety Years of Duke Memorial Church: 1886–1976* (Durham, NC: Duke Memorial United Methodist Church, 1977), 22.

2. Bill Hybels, *Courageous Leadership* (Grand Rapids, MI: Zondervan, 2002, 2009), 32–50.

3. John P. Kotter, "What Leaders Really Do," *Harvard Business Review* (May–June 1990): 103–11.

4. James M. Kouzes and Barry Z. Posner, *The Leadership Challenge*, 3rd ed. (San Francisco: Jossey-Bass, 2002). See chapter 5, "Envision the Future," 109–40.

5. Ronald A. Heifetz and Marty Linsky, *Leadership on the Line: Staying Alive through the Dangers of Leading* (Boston: Harvard Business Review Press, 2002), 13–20.

6. John P. Kotter, *Leading Change* (Boston: Harvard Business Review Press, 1996), 71–80.

7. Bill Easum, *Unfreezing Moves: Following Jesus into the Mission Field* (Nashville: Abingdon, 2001), 47–52. See also Robert Schnase, *Just Say Yes! Unleashing People for Ministry* (Nashville: Abingdon, 2015).

8. Paul D. Borden, *Direct Hit: Aiming Real Leaders at the Mission Field* (Nashville: Abingdon, 2006), 147.

9. www.pghopendoor.org.

3. EYES WIDE OPEN

1. Parker J. Palmer, *Let Your Life Speak: Listening for the Voice of Vocation* (San Francisco: Jossey-Bass, 2000), 88.

2. Karl Weick, qtd. in *Strategy Bites Back: It Is a Lot More, and Less, Than You Ever Imagined*, ed. Henry Minztberg, Bruce Ahlstrand, and Joseph Lampel (Upper Saddle River, NJ: FT Press, 2005), 69–70.

3. Eugene H. Peterson, *The Contemplative Pastor: Returning to the Art of Spiritual Direction* (Grand Rapids, MI: Eerdmans, 1989), 61.

4. Luke Timothy Johnson, *Scripture and Discernment: Decision Making in the Church* (Nashville: Abingdon, 1996), 14.

5. Ibid.

6. On coming to clarity see Danny E. Morris and Charles M. Olson, *Discerning God's Will Together: A Spiritual Practice for the Church* (Herndon, VA: Alban, 2012), 65–67.

7. Alan Roxburgh and Fred Romanuk, *The Missional Leader: Equipping Your Congregation to Reach a Changing World* (San Francisco: Jossey-Bass, 2006), 87.

8. Roxburgh and Romanuk call this the phases of coming to understanding and applying evaluation. See *The Missional Leader*, 91–96.

9. Morris and Olson, *Discerning God's Will Together*, 76–77.

10. Most models of discernment planning have much in common. The above discussion was significantly influenced by Roxburgh and Romanuk, *The Missional Leader*, especially chapter 5; Morris and Olson, *Discerning God's Will Together*; and Elizabeth Liebert, *The Soul of Discernment: A Spiritual Practice for Communities and Institutions* (Louisville: Westminster John Knox, 2015), 139–55, especially her emphasis on ongoing evaluation.

11. Russ S. Moxley, *Becoming a Leader Is Becoming Yourself* (Jefferson, NC: McFarland, 2015), 162.

12. Ibid., 163.

13. Peter Block, *Community: The Structure of Belonging* (San Francisco: Berrett-Koehler, 2009), 85–92.

4. MISSION AND EVANGELISM

1. Dr. Peter Storey, "The Local Church in Ministry to God's World" (class, Duke Divinity School, Durham, NC, September 2, 1999).

2. Dr. Theodore O. Wedel, a former Canon of the Washington National Cathedral in Washington, DC, wrote this parable in 1953. Ordained as an Episcopal priest in 1931, he served for a time as president of the Episcopal Church's House of Deputies.

3. Scott Jones, *The Evangelistic Love of God & Neighbor* (Nashville: Abingdon, 2003), 23.

4. David J. Bosch, "Evangelism: Theological Currents and Cross-currents Today," *International Bulletin of Missionary Research* (July 1987), 103.

5. Annysa Johnson, "Pastor from Farm Country Takes to Front Lines of Milwaukee Urban Tensions," *Milwaukee Wisconsin Journal Sentinel*, September 2, 2014, http://archive.jsonline.com /news/religion/pastor-from-farm-country-takes-to-front-lines-of -milwaukee-urban-tensions-b99340482z1-273595001.html.

6. William H. Lamar, IV, interview with the author, [June 30, 2016].

7. David Kinnaman and Gabe Lyons, *Good Faith: Being a Christian When Society Thinks You're Irrelevant* (Grand Rapids, MI: Baker Books, 2016), 12.

8. Michael Lipka, "Major U.S. Metropolitan Areas Differ in Their Religious Profiles," *Pew Research Center*, July 29, 2015, www .pewresearch.org/fact-tank/2015/07/29/major-u-s-metropolitan -areas-differ-in-their-religious-profiles/.

9. Thomas Schlesinger, "1500 Hear Dr. Rustin In Farewell Sermon," *The Washington Post*, September 18, 1950.

10. Jim Wallace, foreword to *By Grace Transformed: Christi-*

anity for a New Millennium, by N. Gordon Cosby (Washington, DC: The Potter's House Bookservice Publication, 2005), ix.

11. Michelle Boorstein, "Activist D.C. Church Embraces Transition in Name of Its Mission," *The Washington Post*, January 6, 2009, www.washingtonpost.com/wp-dyn/content/article /2009/01/05/AR2009010503341.html.

12. N. Gordon Cosby, *By Grace Transformed* (Washington, DC: The Potter's House Bookservice Publication, 2005), 10.

13. John Alexander, *Being Church* (Eugene, OR: Cascade Books, 2012), 109.

14. Samuel Wells, *A Nazareth Manifesto* (Chichester, UK: Wiley Blackwell, 2015), 44.

5. GIVING OUR BEST

1. http://angusbarn.com/philosophy.html.

2. Personal conversation with Stanley Hauerwas.

3. Kirsten Akens, "Nadia Bolz-Weber's Good News," *Colorado Springs Independent*, April 15, 2015, www.csindy .com/coloradosprings/pastor-nadia-bolz-webers-good-news /Content?oid=3024026.

4. Amy Butler in an interview with the author.

5. Jim Collins, *Good to Great* (New York: HarperCollins, 2001), 41.

6. Ibid., 127.

6. PRESENT YOUR BODIES

1. Anthony B. Robinson, *Transforming Congregational Culture* (Grand Rapids, MI: Eerdmans, 2003), 43–44.

2. Ibid., 46.

3. Tex Sample, *Blue Collar Resistance and the Politics of Jesus* (Nashville: Abingdon, 2006), 51–53.

4. Shane Hipps, *Flickering Pixels: How Technology Shapes Your Faith* (Grand Rapids, MI: Zondervan, 2009), 76.

5. Stephen Fowl, *Philippians* (Grand Rapids, MI: Eerdmans, 2005), 88.

7. BETTER TOGETHER

1. Eugene Peterson, *The Pastor: A Memoir* (New York: HarperOne, 2012), 277.

2. Ibid.

3. Ibid., 279.

4. Russ S. Moxley, *Becoming a Leader Is Becoming Yourself* (Jefferson, NC: McFarland, 2015), 22.

5. Barbara Kellerman, *The End of Leadership* (New York: Harper Business, 2012).

6. Ibid., 23.

7. Ibid., 42.

8. Ibid., 47.

9. Ronald A. Heifetz and Marty Linsky, *Leadership on the Line: Staying Alive through the Dangers of Leading* (Boston: Harvard Business Review Press, 2002), 123.

10. Ibid., 101–22.

11. Jenny Williams, "How Baptism Makes My 'Job Description' Different," *Pastoral Work: Engagements with the Vision of Eugene Peterson*, eds. Jason Byassee and L. Roger Owens (Eugene, OR: Cascade Books, 2014), 178.

12. Don Cousins, *Experiencing Leadershift: Letting Go of Leadership Heresies* (Colorado Springs: David C. Cook, 2008), 142, 227ff.

13. Ibid., 126–47.

14. Roger heard Don Cousins offer this advice at an event in Raleigh, North Carolina, when he was speaking about his book, *Leadershift*.

CONCLUSION

1. www.oxforddictionaries.com/definition/desperation.

APPENDIX

1. Many of the suggestions in this appendix are our distillations and adaptation of the wisdom in Peter Block's *Community: The Structure of Belonging* (San Francisco: Berrett-Koehler, 2008, 2009). If there is a "next book" to read, Block's is it.

2. For more on "turning to wonder," see The Center for Courage and Renewal at www.couragerenewalorg/turning-to-wonder/.

CPSIA information can be obtained
at www.ICGtesting.com
Printed in the USA
LVOW13s1921290317
528961LV00010B/15/P